Unreasonable Doubt

Unreasonable Doubt

Real Story

Essam M. Al Mohandis

PARTRIDGE
A Penguin Random House Company

To order additional copies of this book, contact
Toll Free 800 101 2657 (Singapore)
Toll Free 1 800 81 7340 (Malaysia)
orders.singapore@partridgepublishing.com

www.partridgepublishing.com/singapore

Contents

Dedication and Appreciation...vii

Preface ix

Good-bye, Boston 1

The Events that Took Place before Leaving to the
United States.. 11

Leaving to King Khalid's International Airport in Riyadh......... 16

Flying on a German Airline 19

A Story at Frankfurt Airport...21

An Ambush at Logan International Airport..............................26

The Customs Hall and Bitterness of Suffering..........................29

Investigation and the Slander Play..35

Saturday's Bleak Events Roll...46

Falsified Witness 57

Release Conditions and Return Home 77

How Things Are Inside a Plymouth County
Correctional Facility (PCCF)..80

Patty Saris, the Judge 87

Friday, January 23, 2004..89

Temporary Residence...96

The First Meeting with Conrad at the Federal Defense Office 102

Shopping and an Unexpected Visit 107

Looking for a Less Expensive Apartment and Meeting
    the Attorney 111

The First Day: The Beginning of the Court 124

The Second Day: The Witnesses 130

The Third Day: Litigations Continue 136

The Fourth Day of the Court 144

The Case at the Hands of the Jury: The Carrier of the
    Glad Tidings 148

The Second Arrest: What Happened? 154

Returning to the Homeland 159

Special Thanks 163

Dedication and Appreciation

The sun of truth rose and shined clearly. I could see and feel the bounties of God, Lord the Almighty, in all that had happened and transpired. Hence, I would like to express my gratitude and appreciation to everyone who participated in making these events happen and contributed to the rising of the sun and enabling of this book to see the light of the vast horizon. I humbly present this effort (this book), which I spent five consecutive years writing and editing. I would like to mention here the following persons:

- My grandfather, the engineer of late King Abdulaziz Kingdom of Saudi Arabia founder's, may God the Almighty shower both of them with His mercy
- My grandmother, may God the Almighty shower her soul with His mercy
- Both of my dear and beloved parents
- HRH Prince Mohammed bin Nayef, KSA interior minister
- My dear and beloved wife Um-Mohammed
- My wife's father Musa'ed AlRayhan
- My wife's uncle Saud AlRayhan
- My Uncles Saud, Khalid, and Abdurrahman and all of my aunts
- My dear and beloved brother Yousef and my brothers and sisters
- Ms. Miriam Conrad, the disciplined and proficient attorney

- Mr. Andy Pevehouse, the disciplined and proficient attorney (Ms. Conrad's former assistant in 2003)
- My sincere friends, especially Engineer Ossama 'Abbass, Engineer Mohammed AlHayyan, and Mr. As'ad AlRayyes
- My sincere and loyal friends and colleagues in both departments of clinical engineering and medical laboratories at King Faisal Specialist Hospital & Research Center
- All my neighbors and beloved ones

I also thank everyone who extended any virtual act, of course, after the due virtues of God the Almighty to produce this book in the best shape and form. Also, thanks to those who participated in the review, offered an opinion, and added or omitted a word that improved the book in general in order to make the book appear in its beautiful shape. To all of you, I say, "Thank you."

On top of this list of the people to be thanked and appreciated are the following:

- Dr. AbdulRahman bin Saleh Al'Ashmawee, the renowned thinker, writer, and poet
- Mr. Salah AlQain, Biometrics Department at King Faisal Specialist Hospital & Research Center Sinor Biostatistician
- Ruqayyeh AlMohandis, my paternal aunt and Arabic language supervisor

I seek God's pardon and forgiveness for all those whom I forgot to mention by name, even though they extended a helping hand to me while doing the work on this book. I'm sure that God the Almighty would not forget such people from His reward.

Preface

This is amazing ….

First and last, all praise is due to God the Almighty. May His peace and blessings be onto His slave-servant messenger Mohammed, the most honorable amongst His prophets and messengers. Yes, it is amazing. I did not find a word after I read this book except this word. This is amazing.

It is a reality like that which is imaginary or virtual reality. It takes place under the sight of "democracy," and it hears about it. It takes place on its own land. It runs through its own civilized and developed human society's blood vessels.

Yes, it is amazing. This is really amazing. It uncovers the snake's holes and pits of the scorpions and serpent. It opens the windows to uncover the light of the truth through what is hidden behind the claims' walls, the illusions of *The Corridors of Injustice*, and the darkness of galleries.

This is really amazing. Essam Almohandis, the writer of these pages, is a young Arab Muslim with bright hope and a clear goal of work away from the paths of illusion. He is extremely keen to practice and implement the principle that states, "A sign of good practices of a person is to leave out what does not concern him."

I'm here not to say good things about him or commend him before God the Almighty, but I merely describe his condition. Yet he faced hard difficulties in that remote place, those that are only suitable for a serious and stubborn criminal.

This is really amazing. I will not cover what triggered my amazement in this book. The book is the experience, sufferings, and crystal clear truth without any ambiguity or vagueness. You should see that for yourself, as I felt and saw.

Essam had conveyed to us the minute details of that truth in a distinct, beautiful, and clear style. The one thing remaining for the reader is to read thoroughly with full awareness and insight. Awareness is the missing diamond for many Muslims at this age and time.

My greetings and salute to the writer as well as the reader and to every line of this book.

AbdulRahman Saleh AlAshmawee, Poet and Thinker

Good-bye, Boston

Final Moments, Sad Memories, and a Return to the Dearest Homeland

It was Saturday, February 28, 2004. The clock hands pointed to 9:00 a.m. in Logan International Airport in Boston, Massachusetts. The external temperature was below zero Centigrade. The sun did not rise this morning. The police officer released me from my shackles and handcuffs. I sat waiting on one of the chairs in one of the airport terminals.

I discovered the truthfulness of the prosecutor and fulfillment of his promise, as he told me yesterday. He would try to deport me as soon as possible to my homeland. I discovered the human side of his personality. A person who sees a prosecutor in court trying by all possible means to prove the accusations and pin them to me would not see the same person who visited me yesterday in the deportation jail. He was totally a different person. He was a kind man, he dealt nicely with me. While I was having mixed feelings of happiness, worries, and lack of reassurance, the kind old customs officer approached me with a greeting.

"Good morning."

"Good morning to you, oh good man."

"Congratulations for gaining back your freedom and innocence. I was sure that you were innocent."

"Thanks for your good feelings and wishes. You are a real gentleman."

"Can I help you?"

"I'm supposed to depart today for my home country, but I don't know the departure time. Can you call the prosecutor and get the accurate information from him?"

"Do you have his contact number?"

"Yes, I do. Here it is. Thank you very much for being so kind."

I handed the Old customs officer's the business card of the prosecutor, which he had given me personally when he visited me last night in the deportation jail. This kind man's wonderful feelings and kind words helped cure some of my unhealed wounds. I thank you. You are truly a kind man. Your attitudes with me relate the Western humanitarian feelings to me. They clearly say that he is one thing and his system is another.

Only a few moments passed before the arrival of the old man who brought along two donuts. "Here is your donut. I shall bring you a cup of hot coffee."

"Thank you, oh good man. I'm fasting today in thanks and appreciation to Almighty God. I thank Him for His grace. The *Boston Herald* did an interview with me for the newspaper. Is it possible to get a copy of the newspaper?"

"It's my pleasure."

That good man left the scene and came back with the newspaper article. "Your picture looks wonderful."

"Thank you. Thank you."

"The prosecutor informed me that he will come to the airport at two O'clock and the plane will leave at three. Do you need anything else?"

"I can't thank you enough, my good man."

"Don't worry about it. Good-bye."

"Good-bye."

At 11:00 a.m., I went with one man, an airport worker who asked me to cooperate with him. Again, he asked me a few more repeated questions that left me bored. He jotted down my answers on his desktop computer. After he concluded his questions, he printed them, along with my answers, on a sheet of paper. He requested me to read them and sign at the bottom of the paper. I could have refused to do so or even objected and asked for my attorney's presence, but I did not. The truth was crystal clear, as strong as the shining sun. I didn't have anything to hide. When he took my fingerprints, he asked me another silly question. I did not hide my laughter.

He asked if I'd like to ask for political asylum or go back home. I answered him sincerely. I would rather go home. Upon hearing that, he shamefully put down his head as he heard my truthful and decisive words. They were very frank and open. They revealed the feelings of a person who loved his country, his homeland, and his family and believed in his faith, principles, and doctrine.

I sat down on one of the seats outside his office after offering my prayer. It was 1:30 p.m. I looked at the incoming passengers and customs inspectors as they inspected some of the passengers' luggage.

While doing so, the old man who worked in the customs office, wearing his civilian attire, came toward me. "You look more elegant in civilian attire."

"I don't know what to say."

"I'm sure you've passed through difficult times and bad people. Believe me, there are good people in this country."

"I believe you are one of them. I only carry tolerance in my heart despite all the difficulties I went through personally and caused my family members, children, and friends to endure. My good man, in this world, there are human-soul roses and thorns, there are good and evil. I believe that whatever happened to a person in this life is good for him or her. If one is bestowed a grace upon, one would be thankful. And if one is inflicted with hardships and difficulties, one would be patient, which is good for him."

The old man extended his hand sadly to shake hands with me. "Be good and safe."

"I hope to meet you in better circumstances. I wish you all the best from the bottom of my heart."

The old man said good-bye to me and left, but the years to come would never erase his good treatment from my memory. Yes, kind man, you can't really tell the sad situation of my parents, wife, brothers, paternal and maternal uncles and aunts, the rest of my brothers and sisters, and my extended family members. They were upset day and night. They exerted every effort, offering supplications to God the Almighty to ease my situation. They cried a lot. They all had broken hearts.

Yet they demonstrated a high level of patience and perseverance. They entrusted God the Almighty with all our affairs. They were sure that I was innocent and I would come back home soon, safe and sound. They were truthful with God the Almighty, and He was also truthful with them. They were able to see me back among them. All praise is due to God the Almighty.

From a distance, I could see the prosecutor stepping toward me. It was 2:15 p.m. He had my traveling ticket, my passport, my wallet, my coat, and a message from my beloved wife in his hand. She assured me that everything was well with her and her father. The prosecutor handed me a copy of her and her father's reservations. The departure date was the next day, Sunday.

Glorified be the Almighty God. My wife and her father came to the United States with the hope and intent to travel back along with me. But there I was, leaving them unwillingly. At that time, my heart wept silently. I'd been parted from the person I loved, with whom I'd spent the best days of my life. She was the one of whom I have the best hopes, dreams, and memories.

The prosecutor said good-bye to me and wished me a pleasant trip. At the gate for my plane, an official handed me my passport, along with my tickets. My destination was Frankfurt, Germany. My flight was on Lufthansa Airlines. I'd begin my journey toward my beloved homeland, my beloved country, the Kingdom of Saudi

Arabia. I would end up in Riyadh with a stopover in the city of Jeddah, the bride of the Red Sea.

I sat in my assigned seat in the plane. When the passengers were all seated, the plane headed toward the runway. Our speed accelerated with the beats of my own heart. Joy and exhilaration appeared on my face. The plane's wheels gradually left the runway, and we rose up through the clouds. I continued looking at the city of Boston, which looks at the Atlantic Ocean. I tried to examine some of its landmarks and features. I could see the John Joseph Moakley United States Courthouse, which is close to the airport. I could also see the Federal Defender Office.

I noticed the streets crowded with cars and trucks. It was very cold, but the warmth of my feelings overpowered the coldness of the place around me. Only twenty-four hours ago, I was shuttling between the court and the federal defendant's office, not knowing how my case would end. But now in my hand, I carried a letter that stated my innocence from all accusations. I had no luggage and no backpack.

Trying times and difficult situations reflect the reality of people. Their actions prove their realities. How many times had a friend claimed a true friendship to me but proved to me that he was otherwise during trying times? In contrast, others proved their truthfulness, loyalty, and devotion. I had seen with my own eyes the one who came personally to Boston for my support. He had given his testimony in my favor before the court. He left his work and family behind for my sake. I had seen some people who tried their best to travel before February 23, 2004, the beginning of the court date, but the security claims of the embassy and security hysterical call, prevented him from doing so. He was subject to injustice, cancellation of his entry visa to the United States, and exposure of himself for imprisonment.

I had seen the truthfulness of people who mixed their voices with their tears for my sake every time they called me on the phone. Their words were healing ones. Their supplications supported me, and I had noticed the impact of their true petitions on my case . All praise is due to God the Almighty, who enabled me to have such sincere and loyal brethren, whether I knew them or not. I ask God the Almighty to give them the greatest of rewards and bless their hearts.

A German passenger sitting next to me disrupted my chain of thoughts. He studied his bachelor's, master's, and PhD in neurosciences in Boston. He worked as a researcher at Massachusetts Institute of Technology (MIT), one of the renowned advanced schools in the world. He spoke to me, not knowing who I was nor the circumstances I passed through.

The German scientist became bored and tired of the tremendous security procedures in the United States. Just a short while ago, he received an offer to work in his own country. He was going there to discuss the details. He said he would not return to Boston if he agreed with them on the offer.

This German scientist would give up his career in Boston, where he lived, breathed its air, and loved the people whom he worked with. He shared with me his worries and concerns about the scientific and technical advanced future for the United States in general and Boston in particular.

Not a single corner or side of the city of Boston lacks an institute, college, or university whose students come from all over the world. The September 11 events and hallucinations of the administration of the president of the United States turned away many willing students to come and study in the United States to come there. Rather, many of the new students changed their directions to study in Europe, the United Kingdom, and Australia. This would surely negatively affect the economical aspect of the United States, and it would have a bearing on the "brain migration" from the United States as well.

I listened very carefully to what the German scientist had to say. I admired his way of thinking, discussion, deep vision, and detailed analysis. We spent some time talking about Germany as an industrial state. We addressed his records of achievements. We talked about the social structure of the German society and community as compared with the American counterpart. We talked about the disunion, disconnection, and incoherence of the family in the United States. We tackled many issues and talked about a wide range of subjects.

After more than nine hours of continuous flight, we arrived at the German territories. We passed over Switzerland and France. The plane landed at Frankfurt. We disembarked the plane, and I headed to the transit hall where the Saudi Airlines office is located. The time according to my wristwatch was 7:00 a.m. Frankfurt local time, on Saturday, February 28, 2004 .

Eight more hours remained for the departure of the flight heading to Jeddah. I went to a store and bought a calling card. I called my parents, brother, and my wife and her father as well. I also bought a newspaper to pass some time and learn about the news. I was disconnected from the world for almost two months in a country that makes and fabricates the news.

I sat down and reviewed the touching tape of memories that took place in a stage of my life. The successive events went on continuously with all their sufferings, surprises, and its divine facilitation. Hours passed, and I did not feel what was going on around me. I was drowned in the ocean of painful memories and lonesome darkness of injustice.

My goodness. I couldn't believe what happened. Every time I moved from one point to the next on the memory's tape, I thanked God the Almighty for His kindness, uncountable graces, and benevolence in facilitating and easing my affairs.

* * *

My memories took me back to 10:00 p.m. on Monday, December, 29, 2003. On that same night God the Almighty blessed me with my first daughter.

The next day, I met my boss, Engineer Abdullah. He congratulated me for the baby girl and further told me that another surprise was waiting for me. He informed me about a trip to the United States. The exclusive representative of the American company in Riyadh set the training date on the DNA replicate device. The date would be two days from that time, if I accepted the traveling idea as per the offered training schedule. In fact, I liked the idea without any hesitation. The training period was relatively short, nine days. My wife would spend some time with her family, forty days post birth, as is the traditions in our culture.

I missed the first training date for this course, which was on December 6, 2003. I applied to the US Embassy in Riyadh in July 2003.

A middle-aged lady in her forties received my application.

"What is the reason of your visit to the United States?"

"Training on a machine purchased by the hospital I work in."

"What is the name of the company that would provide the training? What are the applications or uses of the machine?"

"It is an American company that manufactures modern technological machines that replicate the DNA, hereditary tape, in the field of medical diagnosis."

"Did you visit the United States in the last ten years?"

"No, I didn't visit it absolutely."

"Are you married? How many children do you have?"

"Yes. I have two children."

"The embassy may request you to come again for another interview. Do you have any objection?"

"Of course not. I am ready to answer any further or additional questions or supply any further documents or information."

"You have to understand that submitting an application to the embassy does not necessarily mean it is accepted. It might take approximately six to eight weeks to get the reply from the secretary of state (Ministry of Foreign Affairs) in the United States and the authorities of the Homeland Security."

"But my training date is approximately after five weeks."

"I can't accelerate this process. Your documents would be submitted through the normal channels and according to the instructions that we have in the embassy."

Days passed by. The training date was due. There was no news yet from the US Embassy about the visa. After five weeks, I received a call from Basel, an employee in the US Embassy. He requested I come to the embassy after the fasting month holidays. I went to the US Embassy as requested and submitted my passport. I asked about the employee Basel, but no one apparently knew him.

But another employee there informed me that the instructions were given to issue me an entry visa to the United States. The visa was valid for one year from the issuing date. The employee received my passport and informed me to come back after one week to get the visa.

It was the Almighty God's wisdom that my wife agreed with me, after a lot of hesitation, to attend the training during that time for two reasons. First, it was to benefit from the scientific and professional training opportunity in order to better serve the generous and beloved country. She realizes my passion and strong enthusiasm for my work. She also realizes my strong desire to improve my professionalism and deepen my knowledge about my career.

Second, she realizes my passion for travel and widening my cognizance. She usually repeats the proverb that says, "Travel has seven benefits," yet I am still looking into the benefits of travel and, in particular, the first benefit, despite the passing of years.

My newborn daughter Wasan was like her elder brother Mohammed and all other children. She slept during the daytime and woke up at night. Of course, parents complain a lot about this habit. Further, her mother didn't like that habit at all. This also bothered me as I had a full-time job that required focus and attention. Of course, this did not meet the liking of our beloved newborn daughter Wasan. She screamed from the top of her lungs right next to my ears.

On the morning of January 2, 2004, I received a call from Engineer Mohammed, whose company represented the American company in my beloved country, the Kingdom of Saudi Arabia. He informed me that he arranged all the hotel reservations and he was waiting for the air tickets confirmation. He said he would tell me as soon as he would receive the air tickets.

On that same night, my family and I sat at home expecting the arrival of my colleague at work, Engineer Ossama 'Abbass, along with his family. Engineer Ossama was a colleague and previous boss. We worked together for eight years previously. We have a strong bond of friendship that ties us together. Engineer Ossama was distinguished for his work in the fields of clinical engineering and information technology as well. This led him to develop an ecosystem under the name of "Reengineering of Process and Supply Chain Management in the Health-care Arena."

This ecosystem was known as part of the EGovernment in the health sector, which saves the Saudi government over $4 million (US) annually. Local Saudi newspapers and media commended Engineer Ossama's contributions.

I received a call from the representative of the US company about 5:30 p.m. He informed me that he would like to arrange a time to hand me the air tickets along with the hotel reservations. He wished me a safe and happy journey, along with good scientific benefits from the training course.

The Events that Took Place before Leaving to the United States

I drove quickly to go home. As soon as I got there and parked my car, I noticed my wife's uncle, Mr. Saud Abu Rayhan, his wife, his son, and his son-in-law. All the children, including my own son, were playing joyfully at the time. They were in and out of the living room and the ladies' section. They played innocently and had great fun. We heard them chanting, singing, and playing cheerfully. Their joyful screams filled the home and hearts with joy and happiness.

After a short time only, the guests sought permission to leave one after the other. The time passed so quickly. It is true that time flies when you are having fun. I headed to the bedroom. The time was 10:00 p.m. Tomorrow was Friday. My wife, her mother, and my two children were supposed to leave the city, and I was supposed to leave to the United States.

I tossed around on my bed. While doing so, my imagination took me to the United States. The company's engineer informed me that the weather in Boston was too cold. In fact, he said that snow covered the entire city at times. I imagined myself rolling on the layers of snow. I remembered my reverend professor, Dr. Ahmad Nasef. May God shower him with His mercy. And I thought of his lengthy talks about the United States and its people. He lived in Houston, Texas. He was truly in love with that city, where he died before the events of September 11, 2011.

I looked at the weather forecast for the next five days on the Internet. Although the forecast was for pretty cold weather, lots of snow, frost, and freezing situation, I was still happy and excited. While going through such imaginations, I fell in a deep and quiet sleep.

I woke up at the prayer call. It was a new day. I had a strange feeling of depression. I could not breathe. I did not know the reason for such a depressing feeling. After sunrise, I headed to the gravesite of both my grandparents in Riyadh Cemetery. I don't know what urged me to do so, but I cried very hard until I sobbed. I never cried so hard for a long time before. I stood by the graveside and had flashes about their memories and my life that I spent with them.

My brother Yousef, who is one year younger than I am, and I lived close to them. They loved us so much. We also loved them very much. They had offered us very special tender care. They offered us unmatchable love and immeasurable attention. Our requests were all fulfilled. All we needed was brought immediately. We were treated with true love, and we were really spoiled. Yet, we were given every good, truthful, and kind advice and direction.

I went back to the house. I prepared myself for Friday prayer. I went to the mosque to offer my prayers. Yet, I was still feeling uptight, uncomfortable, and somewhat depressed. My chest was so tight as if my ribs were about to crack.

What is the matter with me? I feel depressed for no reason.

As if my heart is becoming stranger of its own time.[1] I walked after the Friday prayer to my father's home. I wanted to say good-bye to him. I sat with my father in private in his room.

He said, "I wish you wouldn't go to the United States. The situations there are neither smooth nor settled." But he retracted what he said. "If this trip is not in your country's favor to better serve your country, I would not have allowed you to travel. Son, be super careful."

---

[1]   A poem by Mohammed Hasan Awwad

I wondered why my father said what he did. This was not the first time I traveled to a Western country after September 11. I had traveled to Holland, Germany, and Japan, and he never offered such a strong advice before.

I intended to tell him, "But, Dad, would you like me to cancel the training or maybe postpone it to a different date?"

But I didn't. I didn't know what made me not say anything. Yet my father wished me well and prayed for me. I kissed my father's head and hand, as it is our tradition. I asked God the Almighty to preserve him and grant him a long, happy life. My young brothers surprised me with a pleasant gift, a copy of the Glorious Quran. I thanked them for this great gift and their kindness. I sought permission to leave. The events in general were normal. But deep in my heart, I still felt uptight. I did not know the reason for such a feeling. Events then after went so quickly in a way that I never experienced before.

I headed home to drive my wife, her mother, and my two children to the airport to catch their flight to the city of Taief, where her family lives. My wife noticed the change in my behavior. She further noticed that I was spaced out. She read that on my face. Everyone got in the car, and I drove them to the airport. I put their suitcases on the trolley and pushed it through the hall. I walked them to the last point by the entrance to the gateway.

My wife usually turns toward me one last time again before she leaves to go to the boarding gate, but she did not do so this time. I thought she might be busy with her newborn baby girl. But it was not the reason, as she told me about it later in Boston.

I drove back to my father's home. That coming Sunday would be the seventh day after the birth of Wasan. It would be time for a tradition to be done on her behalf on that day. Muslims slaughter one lamb on the seventh day of the birth of a baby girl and two lambs for a baby boy. They cook them and offer a thankfulness or thanksgiving party to God the Almighty.

I wanted to request my father to do so on my behalf. He just came back from the *Masjid* after offering his late evening prayer, there. He was surprised to see me again since I said good-bye to him on the afternoon of the same day. My father stood at the entrance of the house and gave me a special look. I didn't know the interpretation of that look until later when I reached the United States.

I went home, but as soon as I entered the house, I felt strangely lonesome. In fact, this is the case when I come home and my wife and beloved children Mohammed and Wasan are not here. The house was deeply quiet as if no children were playing and chanting last night. The house, in fact, is not mere furniture and décor. The real beauty of a home is its tenants, my wife and two children. The house was totally empty except for their memories. A toy for my son Mohammed was on the floor. On the other side of the room, there was a crib for my daughter Wasan. A few things of my wife's were scattered here and there in the house. This reminded me with a poem of a modern Arab poet that goes as follows:

Where is the beautiful noise? Where is the commotion?
Where is the pretend study, mixed with play?
Where is the childish behavior at its peak?
Where are the toys on the floor and where
are the scattered books all over?
Where are the complaints for no reason?
Where is the needless quarrel?
Where are the cries and laughter, together?
Where are the sadness and the joy?
Their i.e. the children chanting is Papa, if they are happy.
And they cry Papa again, if they wanted to threaten one another.
They call Papa if they go away.
They also call Papa if they were close.
Only Yesterday they filled our house.
And today, what a day. They are all gone.
Yes. They did go indeed.
But, in the heart they reside regardless where they go, far or near.
I could see feel them everywhere.
Whether moving or still.
Even if they left the house they pulled away my heart with them.
They pulled away my beating heart from its caging ribs.
You could see me emotionally like a child.
Crying like a pouring rain.
Blamers may wonder about a crying man …
In fact, they should wonder if I don't.
I wish all the crying is an indication of weakness.
But, though I am a strong man, I am still a father.[2]

---

[2] Omar Bahaa AlAmeeree, an Arab Islamic poet

Leaving to King Khalid's International Airport in Riyadh

My beloved wife prepared my travelling clothes and backpack, as she always does two days before the departure. I took a warm shower, put on my clothes, carried my backpack, and headed to my oldest paternal aunt to say good-bye to her. I did not find her at home, but I found my other aunt. I told her to say good-bye on my behalf to my parental uncles and aunts. From there, I went to the hospital where I work because some of our colleagues wanted to join us to the airport. On the way, I called my wife and made sure that all reached well and safely.

It was almost 9:00 p.m. I waited for almost thirty minutes for my colleague, Engineer Ossama Abbass. I remembered then that I left my travelling camera that accompanies me on my trips. I wanted to take it with me to the United States for photos and videos shots that I keep for memory sake.

I had left my little backpack inside my car, which I parked in the hospital's parking lot. Thus, I headed toward my home in Engineer Ossama's car. I did not stay long. I picked up my camera, and we left. We went to the hospital again to meet my colleagues. I met Engineer Mohammed AlHayyan and Engineer Faisal AlFarisi. We sat together and chatted for a short while. As per our agreement, we would go together to King Khalid International Airport. But Engineer Ossama remembered that he had another appointment that he had to attend to. We said good-bye to him, and he left.

Engineer AlFarisi drove us in his car to the airport. We said good-bye to him and went to the King Khalid International Airport.

At this point, I again forgot my camera in the car of Engineer AlFarisi. My friend, Engineer AlHayyan, suggested to call Engineer AlFarisi and have him bring it to the airport. But I decided not to do so. Who knows? It might have been a good thing that I forgot the camera again. We headed to the Lufthansa counter at the airport.

I put the luggage on the screening machine. The person in charge directed us to the Lufthansa counter on the opposite side of the hall. Our luggage went for the second time on the screening machine. We requested seats next to each other, but the agent apologized in not being able to fulfill our request because the plane was completely packed. We got our boarding passes. My colleague went with me to the ATM machine because I needed some cash for the trip. Of course, I had my credit cards with me. We headed next to the passport authorities to the gate.

It was 1:30 a.m. As soon as I sat down, I felt very drowsy and dozed off. My colleague, Engineer AlHayyan, did the same as well. I don't like to stay up late at night. I have always preferred to go to bed early and get up early as well. The sound of a security lieutenant police officer who opened my black backpack to inspect it suddenly woke me up.

I gave him a strange look. He didn't wake me up or ask my permission to inspect the backpack. When the officer noticed my situation, he told me that he wanted to inspect the contents of my backpack. I nodded at him, telling him it was okay to do so. I was still drowsy.

Another security officer yelled, "Officer Tariq, do you need any assistance?"

The officer responded negatively while he was still going through my backpack's contents. He did a detailed search with his hands. I was watching him with my drowsy eyes. He took out the instruction manual of the machine I was going to be trained on. He asked me to give him my passport. He asked me where I was heading to exactly.

He jokingly commented, "It is nice that your family name coincides with your profession."

I exchanged smiles with him. He handed me back my passport when he was sure that everything was okay. Then he inspected my colleague's luggage. Then he went on to another passenger and so on.

Flying on a German Airline

The time was 2:45 a.m. It was only a few minutes before announcing the Lufthansa flight. Passengers lined up by the plane entrance gate. My friend and I preferred to wait for a while before boarding the plane rather than standing with a crowded, long queue. After noticing that most passengers had entered the plane, we followed them. We were finally on the plane.

The plane was fully booked. There was no room for my backpack to place in the overhead compartment above my seat. I could only find a room for it approximately five rows away behind my assigned seat. At this point, I could no longer see my colleague, Mr. AlHayyan. His seat was in the back of the plane. Next to me sat a man who looked like a cool and pretty quiet person. He looked like he was from Southeast Asia.

I was still feeling drowsy and fatigued. I rested my body on the seat and went into a deep sleep. When I woke up, I noticed that I almost slept over five continuous hours. I went to the bathroom. On the way back to my seat, I took a glance at my colleague, AlHayyan, on one of the seats behind me.

I approached him with a greeting. I asked how he was doing. He said all was fine. I offered my dawn *Fajr* prayer while sitting in my seat. As soon as I finished my prayers, the stewardess announced breakfast time. With a smile on their faces, the cabin crew did their assigned duties. Some of the passengers were ready to eat breakfast, while others were not aware what they were doing. The Southeast Asian passenger next to me was of the latter type.

I ate my breakfast, drank my coffee, and watched the clouds through the window. The wonderful scene of the sun shining over the clouds was just magnificent. It was just another great sign of God the Almighty. The golden sun rays penetrated the mist of the clouds spreading its wonderful golden rays. I wished I had my camera.

But I thought to myself, *Would my humble camera be able to absorb and capture such a wonderful scene? A human being could only bow down in awe and be amazed with the fascinating creation of God the Almighty. The scene is beyond describing in words.* I could not find any suitable words in my vocabulary to describe the scene and connotation for its meanings. I could only glorify God the Almighty, the Creator and Originator of all beings.

The scene did not last long. The accumulated condensed clouds covered it. There were a thunderstorm and rain showers, and then the sky was pouring. I was sure the earth was extremely thirsty for such a wonderful rain. How lovely. It was just another undescribable scene. It was just beyond words. I could no longer feel the time. It was fantastic.

The captain announced that all passengers must return to their seats in preparation for landing in Frankfurt Airport in Germany.

A Story at Frankfurt Airport

When the plane came to a complete stop, I went to get my personal backpack from the overhead compartment a few seats behind me. I placed my black backpack over my back. I headed toward the plane door. I was about to leave this giant flying bird that carried us over seven hours from Riyadh to Frankfurt, the commercial capital of Germany.

I waited for my colleague, AlHayyan. We went together to the transit hall. We asked a German land crewmember about the planes going to San Francisco, where my colleague, AlHayyan, was going, and the one going to Boston, where I was heading. My colleague had two hours for his connection flight's departure, while my connection flight's departure was after three hours. We went together to the duty-free shop to spend some time there shopping or looking. Although the airport in general was heated, the transit halls were freezing ice-cold.

It was 7:30 a.m. in Germany. The weather fluctuated between cloudy and rainy from time to time. I could see one person running, while another one was jogging. I could also see someone laughing, while another one was talking. What a busy and noisy world.

We passed by gift shops and looked at some jewelry and popular brand-name watches. We talked about the prices, the rise of the Euro, and its continuous rise over the exchange price rate of the US dollar. We remembered our previous trips together to France, Germany, Dubai, and Japan.

In fact, this was the first time we traveled to different destinations. We got used to traveling together because we trekked together many times before. We went through the duty-free shop at the airport. After an hour and thirty minutes, my colleague headed to his gate to catch his flight to San Francisco. I accompanied him to the gate. I still had time for my flight. But I was afraid to miss my way back to my flight's gate. I sought his permission to go back to my gate. I said good-bye to him and wished him a safe and pleasant journey. He did the same to me, and we parted with each other.

I felt tired on my way back to the gate. I headed to the gate of my flight to Boston. I passed through the inspection points. I emptied my pockets, took off my belt, and placed all my belongings on the x-ray machine to be inspected, the sixth inspection machine I went through at the airport, including Riyadh. Finally, I was allowed to go into the waiting area flight's gate. I waited over an hour before the flight was announced.

"Flight number four twenty-two going to Boston on Lufthansa Airlines is now boarding."

It was a direct flight from Frankfurt to Boston's Logan International Airport. Again, I preferred to wait until the crowd was over. According to the official manifest, 345 passengers were on this plane. I picked up my backpack and went through the gate. The crewmembers directed me to my seat. Again, I could not find a place for my backpack in the overhead compartment above my seat. I had to search for an empty space ten rows in front of my seat. My assigned seat was 34J. It was 11:30 a.m. in Germany.

Although the sun had risen, one could not barely see it. It hid behind the clouds. All passengers were seated. The captain apologized for the delay because of the bad weather situations. He informed us about the time of the journey until we reached Boston. It would take approximately eight hours.

The captain was finally given a signal to depart. He set the plane on the runway in preparation to begin the flight in the next few minutes. We'd fly over the Atlantic Ocean. The sky was above us,

and the ocean was beneath us. What a splendid scene. I could not
see it closely. A European lady was sitting next to me by the window.
On my left sat an Afro-Arab young man. I slept enough from Riyadh
to Frankfurt. I pulled out the copy of the Glorious Quran that my
young brothers presented to me as a gift upon departing Riyadh. I
recited until the next mealtime. It was an opportunity for me to talk
to the Afro-Arab young man next to me.

"Good afternoon. My name is Essam. How do you do?"

"Good afternoon to you. Pleased to meet you."

"I work as a biomedical engineer in King Faisal Specialist
Hospital and Research Center in Riyadh, Saudi Arabia."

"I am an attorney. I specialize in reimbursements related to work
injury-related cases."

"I am sure you liked the movie as it was filmed in the court."

"It is true. Where are you from?"

I am from the Kingdom of Saudi Arabia."

"I visited Jeddah in 1994, ten years ago."

"Ten years is a long time. KSA changed a lot during this period.
It is witnessing another great construction boom. If you visit it now,
you would see a completely different picture of what you had seen
then."

"You are making me eager to visit your country again."

"Of course. By all means. You should also be my guest. Where
are you from?"

"I am American. I was born in Boston in 1975. My mom is
Eritrean, who became a naturalized American citizen. She works in
Abidjan as national affairs that take care of the American citizens in
Eretria. I just visited her there and started my return journey home
from Asmara. Egypt, Frankfurt, and then Boston."

"It is surely a tiring trip. As for me, I began my trip from Riyadh
to Frankfurt, and here I am joining you to Boston. I am going to
attend some training on specialized medical equipment."

"I noticed you were reading a book a while ago. Was it the
Glorious Quran?"

"Yes. How did you know it?"

"As I mentioned, my mother lives in a country with a lot of Muslims. I had seen it there."

The stewardess handed us our trays of food. She was nice and friendly with a smile on her face. My companion and I started eating our meals. The European lady was asleep. We got busy eating and stopped talking. While both of us were eating, we talked about King Faisal Specialist Hospital and Research Center, one of the most advanced international medical centers. Most of the medical staff in the hospital is trained in the West in general and in the United States, Canada, and Europe in particular. This great structure holds more than fifty different coherent nationalities, cultures, traditions, and customs that work in an unparalleled beautiful harmony. My American comrade looked overwhelmed with what he heard. He continued to seek more information willingly.

He told me about Boston geography. He mentioned the famous landmarks that I should not miss to visit while there. He talked about Cambridge University, Massachusetts Institute of Technology (MIT), historical museums, tourist attractions, and other centers that provide the visitor with a cultural, historical, and civilizational depth about the city and its population makeup.

He talked a lot about the Big Dig and illustrated that Boston witnessed a great hike in the number of the population and incomers. It faced a great problem of congestion. The people in charge in the municipality reached a decision to dig an underground tunnel to connect the various scattered parts of the city to contribute to the alleviation of the congestion. The cost of this project was over billions (USD). It was the third-largest project in the United States. I was pleased to hear all that information. It looked like I would be busy over the weekend to have an opportunity to visit all such sites and places.

The young American further informed me that Boston is a large city with many educational centers, colleges, and universities. I mentioned to him that I would be checking into a hotel on a street that began with the letter "W," as I forgot the full name of the street. He helped me remember the name by listing a score of streets that begin with "W," but I could not remember the exact name of the street.

I got out of my seat and retrieved my backpack to search for the hotel reservation slip. I handed him the slip, and he promised to show me the place and name of the shuttle that would take me there. He advised me not to take a taxi, as the rates were very high. I appreciated his kindness, advice, and information. I left him to get some rest for the remaining time of the flight.

I prepared myself for the prayer. I offered my prayer again while sitting. I continued to watch the movie on the monitor in front of me. I saw a judge sitting on a high bench with elegant furniture surrounding him. Another desk was beneath the main judge's bench. I noticed the witnesses taking stands on that desk. I was bored with the proceedings of the court in the movie. I wrapped myself with the blanket and went into a semi-sleep situation for about an hour or two at the most.

I woke up on the sound of the stewardess collecting the headphones. The captain announced to the passengers to return to their seats in preparation for landing in Logan International Airport. Boston is on the Atlantic Ocean. The young American turned toward me, pointed through the window to Boston, and explained some of the visible features of the northern and southern parts of the city. The captain did not give us the opportunity to have a panoramic view of the landmarks of the city before landing.

Some airplane captains usually take a short round over the city before they land. Surely, it was a long flight. We flew about eight consecutive hours. As soon as we completed filling the immigration and customs arrival form that the stewardess handed us, the plane landed on the airport runway at exactly 12:35 p.m., Boston's local time.

An Ambush at
Logan International Airport

I agreed with the young American to meet after we passed through the immigration and customs inspections. It was Saturday, January 3, 2004. The time at home was 8:35 p.m. The time zone difference time between Riyadh and Boston is eight hours. I headed to the immigration officer. A long queue was ahead of me, approximately thirty or even forty people. We all lined up under a blue sign that said "Non-American Passengers." Another red sign said "USA Citizens."

The queue progressed in a nice and smooth flow. When I approached the immigration officer's booth, it was about 2:10 p.m. I noticed that the officer would ask the passenger a question or two and take his photo by a fixed digital camera connected to his computer. The officer took an index fingerprint of the left hand of the passenger through a digital scanner. I remembered that I read not too long ago that the American authorities increased the readiness alert situation to the "Orange" code after receiving threats of potential attacks internally and externally.

When my turn came, I went to window five or seven. I can't recall exactly. At this point, I noticed the American young man wasn't standing in the American citizens line. The line had a fewer number of people than ours. Therefore, he completed his arrival check procedures and proceeded to go out much quicker than I did. I handed my passport to the immigration officer who asked me to look to the digital camera fixed on his desk. He asked me to place my left index finger on the fingerprint scanner. The officer asked me to come along with him to complete additional further checkups.

He made a remark saying that my nationality required further additional checking. I accompanied him to another checking area. The officer handed my passport to another agent in an area called the "Secondary Inspection Area." He placed my passport in a yellowish envelope and instructed me to wait until my name was called. I felt hot and took off my coat. I felt tired and hungry.

I said to myself, "Well, I would hope to meet the young American after I complete this stage of checking. I would go to the hotel and rest after this lengthy and exhausting journey."

After waiting for thirty minutes in a small hall that had only few seats and many people standing up waiting to be called, one agent called my name. I reached my backpack and followed him to a small and narrow room. He instructed me to leave my backpack outside the room.

I thought, *Why leave my backpack outside?* I never left my belongings in an open space. Several people were crossing through that hall. *The security people might confiscate the backpack if they noticed it unattended. Wouldn't anyone tamper with the backpack?*

All these thoughts crossed my mind when the officer commanded me to leave my backpack outside the inspection room. I hesitated a lot and thought a lot about it. I was not fully convinced with what the agent commanded me to do. But I did not discuss the matter any further with him or debate it. I followed the commands and instructions. I placed my backpack close to one of the seats in the room and followed the agent. The agent told me that I had to answer some routine questions.

"What is your name?"

"Essam Mohammed AlMohandes."

"How long are you planning to stay in Boston?"

"Nine days. This is my training period, along with two weekends."

"Where would you stay?"

"I would be on Waltham Street."

"You mentioned you are here for specialized training. Where would the training take place?"

"In the company's factory."

"Do you have a contact number where we can reach you if need be?"

"The two trainers of the machine I would be trained on in the company would be there most of the time."

The agent was too slow entering the data in the system. At the end of the interview, he thanked me and wished me a pleasant stay. I cordially thanked him and stood up to leave the room. Before leaving the room, he instructed me to come back again to this office before leaving the United States. He instructed me to turn in the official entry official registration paper that I got from this office.

I jotted down this piece of information in order to remember it later. I wrote down the name and number of that particular office before I left. The agent asked me to go to customs clearance and luggage delivery at the lower level.

The Customs Hall
and Bitterness of Suffering

I hurried toward my coat and backpack. They were as tired as I was. They leaned to one of the seats of the room. I left them for about eight minutes while the agent interviewed me. I still had only a few more minutes to enjoy the scenes of the city that I had enjoyed watching the aerial views before landing. I looked forward to see the snowfall covering the land with a beautiful white coat. I also looked forward to breathing fresh cold air filling my lungs and rejuvenating unlimited freshness and activity in both the body and soul.

I thought, *When I arrive at the hotel, it would be around four o'clock in the afternoon. This would be equivalent to twelve thirty in the afternoon back at home. I'll call my parents and my wife. Then I'll take a quick warm shower and take a nap for an hour or so. Then I'll take a short walk around the hotel's area to discover the area, as it is my habit to do so wherever I go.* I love walking and discovering new things. *I'll call the company and inform them that I had arrived for the training. I would like to learn about the training schedule on the coming Monday.*

I thought about all that and more. *What about the hotel? What about the rooms in the hotel? What about the hotel's services?* I was racing with time in my thoughts. I walked toward the stairway. I climbed down the steps quickly. I thought I was too late for my American friend whom I met on the plane. A voice of an officer wearing a blue uniform—a slim Caucasian with maybe French blood of average height—interrupted my thoughts. He had a smile on his face. I did not feel comfortable with him. He looked at me in a suspicious way and then raised his tone.

"Give me your passport."

"Here it is."

"Follow me."

"Okay."

This inspector walked slowly while I followed him. We passed the inspection belt, which was almost empty. There were he, a few other people in charge, and a small number of passengers who were not stopped by anyone.

"Do you have any other luggage?"

"No."

"Do you carry more than ten thousands dollar cash on you?"

"No."

"Did anyone give you anything to bring to the USA?"

"No. Not at all."

"Why are you visiting the USA?"

"I have training on new equipment for the hospital I work in."

"What is the machine?"

I mentioned the name of the machine and explained some of its theory of operation. I read strange observations and impressions on his face, as if he were hearing about such machine for the first time in his life.

"Do you allow me to inspect your backpack?"

"By all means. Go ahead."

He put on his inspection pair of gloves and pulled a book that I read on the plane, *100 Ideas for Tolerance. Practical Applications for Tolerance. NLP Applications to Improve and Repair the Troubled or Totally Cut Relations.*

I can't forget the strange look on his face again, as if he did not understand anything of what I said to him. He pulled out a hairbrush, a small cream tube, and some flyers about the machine I would be training on. He stared at all these items and placed them all on the inspection belt. He inserted his hand in the front zipper of the backpack and pulled out some medicine that I had. I always take some general medications with me while traveling, such as cold and fever medicine, some vitamins tablets, and so forth. He carefully examined all these items and opened them all. He placed them next to the book, the flyers, the hairbrush, and the cream.

The inspector inserted his hand again inside the black backpack and pulled out three yellow cylindrical tubes. Each one was no longer than one and half inches.

He held one of these tubes. "What are these?"

I was in a state of shock. I did not know what they were. "I think they are crayon pens." I did not know what they were. I moved my hand in the air, representing the movement of a coloring-drawing brush, trying to explain that these were crayon pens.

"I asked you. What are these?" he sharply asked.

He was trying to point out to me that he was not convinced with my response. His method of repeating the question indicated that, I was standing on the other side of the inspection belt with a shocked look on my face. I did not know what to tell him. The inspector was on the other side of the belt.

There was approximately fifty centimeters distance between us. I wanted to grab the sample from his hand to see what it was, but he yelled at me and forbid me to do so. I reached the hotel reservation note to draw or color on it to demonstrate to him that it was a mere coloring material, but I discovered it truly was not an oil coloring item. I raised my eyes to the inspector again to see a more frightening scene. The sample in his hand broke, and a thick, black powder (balls) came out of it.

"For the third time, I ask you to tell me what this material is. Tell me."

I stood speechless. I did not have any reply. His looks were very mad. He almost turned into a savage wolf or a hungry and upset hyena. My feet froze in place. My lips were tightly closed. My eyes were as if they protruded from their cavity. I truly did not know what that item was. At first, I described them to be crayon pen items. What made me think that they were so is the following:

- The outside appearance of the samples very much looked like crayon pen items.
- My wife, an artist, likes to draw and color.

I went far with my imagination with these samples. What is the thick, black powder? Is it a kind of drugs? Is it a hazardous biological material? Under all such weird thoughts, sudden shock and mixed feelings that were beyond my description, the inspector commanded me to stop where I was and not move. He left the scene for few moments and came back with a tall, muscular, red-faced officer who was screaming from the top of his lungs. The new officer on the scene held the sample in his hand, examining it and screaming at me.

"Tell me what this is." He was pointing to the sample on the inspection conveyer belt.

"They look like crayon pen items." I started giving a detailed explanation.

"This is nonsense. These are not crayon pen items. This is nonsense. You are lying to us. I don't believe you." He interrupted me sharply and said in a very loud and intense voice.

I tried to explain or illustrate, but no one gave me a chance to do so. He waved his strong arms before my face. I was truly frightened.

The customs supervisor, the boss of the inspector, ordered me to head to another room after looking at the samples along with other officers, which one broke in the hand of the officer. I walked toward that room while frightened and confused. I was fully taken by fear. My eyes protruded from their cavities, my heartbeat increased, my mouth was dry, and the blood almost froze in my vessels.

I headed to an unknown destiny. The room was not more than three square meters in area. It had an ice-cold steel, long seat and steel table. He ordered a guard to watch me, though I was not even moving.

I sat down on the cold steel seat, and I was about to die from fear. My head was confused with thoughts. I tried to retrace my memories. I thought, *Is what is happening true, or is it a mere nightmare that I would recover from after a short while?*

I remembered the dissatisfaction of my parents with this trip. I remembered my father standing at the gate of the house and his unhappy look at me. Now I was able to understand what it meant. What a scene. What a moment.

I remembered the fears of my beloved wife. I remembered how tight I felt then and how my breath was almost seized. I remembered the tears I shed at my grandparents' graves. The tape of all these events passed in front of my eyes as if I could see it. I was very concerned with what they would do to me. What would happen? I did not know anything, but I was sure I was in trouble. A plight was skillfully arranged against me. I knew that no one else other than God the Almighty would get me out of it.

"I raised my head to the sky, seeking the help and aid from my Lord God the Almighty. Tears were about to pour from my eyes or rather from my heart and all my existence."[3]

While I was suffering of such case of fear and confusion, a customs officer came to me and ordered me to take off my shoes and empty all what was in my pockets on the steel table in front of me. I had the air ticket, my Glorious Quran, the direction compass that gave the direction of Makkah for the prayers, my wallet, my hand wristwatch, my small notebook, my car and home keys in Riyadh City, and my mobile phone. He carefully examined every single item.

The customs inspector left the scene and left the guard watching me. The guard did not leave me a single moment. There was a pistol on his waist, a club, a two-way communication unit, and handcuffs, all to frighten the other party.

---

[3]   Fouad Qandeel, *The Inflected One.*

Their guns, clubs, and handcuffs did not scare me. I don't know. Maybe my copy of the Glorious Quran and my prayer direction compass scared them. These two items are my identification and my direction. I truly wished that he, along with all the others, knew the tolerance of my religion, its simplicity, and its open-heartedness toward others. I truly would like to know what really scared them and frightened them of me.

Investigation and the Slander Play

About 4:00 p.m., a man and a woman entered the room where I was sitting.

"Hello. I am from Immigration and Law Enforcement. This is my colleague. He works with me in the same department.

"Hi."

After answering all her routine questions—my name, the reason for my visit to the United States, and my trip from Riyadh to Boston—and other repeated questions, she told me, "Tell me about the samples that the customs inspector pulled out from your backpack."

"I don't know where they came from. I don't know who placed them in my backpack."

I continued to look at her and her companion, who wrote down everything I had said on a note pad with him.

"Direct your answers to the lady. She is the one who is asking, not me."

He was signaling to me not to look at him at all. What a stiff and cruel treatment. I was talking to them with full innocence. But.

"You had mentioned to the customs inspector that you packed your luggage. Is this true?"

"Absolutely not. I did not mention anything as such. I don't even remember that he asked me about who packed my luggage."

She gave me a strange look. "Who then packed your luggage?"

My wife did. "She packed it two days before the date of the travel."

"Is this your backpack, or does it belong to someone else?"

"It is mine for sure. I absolutely do not borrow backpacks from others. This backpack was with me in several trips before."

"Had you seen those samples before?"

"No. it was the first time I saw such samples."

"Why did you tell the inspector when he asked you about them that they were crayon pen kits?"

"Because they looked like crayon pen kits to me."

"I would like to call either your parents or your wife and family members."

"No. Please do not call them. I prefer you inform the embassy of my country, the Kingdom of Saudi Arabia."

I refused her request to call my parents and my wife. My parents were an old, fragile, and sickly couple. My wife was in her confinement period after delivery. I was sure this type of news would affect all a lot.

At about 7:30 p.m., the FBI investigator came to interrogate with me for the first time. An officer from the state troopers of Massachusetts accompanied them. They all introduced themselves to me while I was still in a state of shock. I could not believe what was happening. I knew I was an engineer who came for a training purpose, and here I was, an accused person being pressured with heavy and psychological stressful interrogations, questions, answers, observation, and close examination.

I wonder what those samples had. Were they dangerous to that extent to cause Customs, Homeland Security, the immigration and FBI officers, and state department police investigating me? The FBI agent handed me a sheet with an advice of rights. He ordered me to read it with a loud voice before all those who were present.

"Do you understand what you had just read?"

"Yes. I fully understand it."

"Now, write down your name next to each paragraph you read."

"Okay."

The advice of rights reads as follows:

> *Before any question is addressed to you, you should*
> *know your rights. You have the right to remain silent.*
> *Anything you say may be used as evidence against you*
> *in court. You have the right to consult an attorney.*
> *You have the right that your attorney attends with you*
> *while being interrogated. If you can't hire an attorney*
> *to defend you, the court would assign an attorney for*
> *you. If you decided to answer the questions posed to*
> *you without an attorney, you may stop answering at*
> *any time.*

I signed next to every phrase I read, and I expressed my willingness to answer any question directed to me. The FBI agent started asking me, and his companion wrote down my answers. Their interrogation lasted for about two hours.

True, I sat somewhat tensed. I do not have any logical interpretation for what was happening to me. *Is it a dream and nightmare? Am I awake and alert?* I was totally shocked, frightened, and confused. I had mixed feelings at that time, which I did not know what they were. *My God. Did those people become crazy? Is it the black buried hatred against* myself?

We were five people, inclusive the guard, in that little room that was no more than three square meters in area. The walls were painted with a yellowish color. The door was grey. The lights were dim daylight. There was a steel table and a steel seat fixed and mounted on the wall. The width of the steel seat was no more than forty centimeters. The length of the seat was no more than one and a half meters. The steel seat was cold, the floor was cold, and they made me take off my shoes.

I felt really cold. I felt almost numb with cold. I became extremely tired and fatigued. It was over nineteen hours among flying time, the wait in the transit hall in Frankfurt Airport, and more than eight hours in Logan International Airport spending time in the immigration, secondary inspection area, customs, and finally the investigators.

The human rights defenders and virtues seekers did not feel anything about this. One after another, they took turns investigating me. I kept telling myself that the truth must appear. They should know that I had nothing to do with these samples. I was sure they would let me go to the hotel. I needed to get some rest. The worst-case scenario would be that they deport me and send me back to my home country. That was the worst-case scenario that crossed my mind.

My goodness. How terrible it is to feel aggression and injustice. I was searching in my memory that was under a severe shock. I felt that the situation was disastrous and the problem was huge. My tears froze in my eyes. I felt suffocated and could not even say any word. I felt shattered and brokenhearted. The investigation was totally stripped from all means of humanitarian feelings.

How could a tired and very fatigued person be investigated for a long time? The FBI investigator was stiff like the steel table and cold like the weather in the investigation room. He had very sharp looks. He frowned all the time, and he was pale in appearance.

"What is your name? How old are you? Where do you work? What is the nature of your job?"

"My name is Essam Mohammed AlMohandiss. My date of birth is Aug 3rd, 1970. I work in King Faisal Hospital and Research Center in Riyadh, the capitol of the Kingdom of Saudi Arabia. My position is a biomedical engineer."

"Do you have any nickname besides your name?"

"No. I never had."

"Are you married? Since when? Do you have any children? How old are they?"

"Yes. I have been married for four years. I have my son Mohammed, who is two years and eight months old, and I have a daughter Wasan, who is only five days old."

"Where did you specialize in biomedical engineering?"

"I studied in King Saudi University in Riyadh."

"You look like you can speak and read English well. Have you ever visited the USA before?"

"No, but all my various stages of study required me to learn English. Furthermore, the hospital I work in employs people from over fifty nationalities, and we all communicate in English."

"So, this is the first time you visited the USA?"

"Yes. It is the first visit."

"Explain the nature of your work as a biomedical engineer and what your specialty means."

"I work in King Faisal Hospital and Research Center. It is a specialized hospital of tertiary care. It has many treatment and diagnostic medical equipment. It requires specialized and highly trained staff to operate and maintain such specialized medical equipment. This is only a part of my role in that position."

"How long have you been working with this hospital?"

"Almost nine years thus far."

"Do you have any aggressive or negative feelings toward the Americans?"

"No."

"Not even the military staff?"

"No."

"Are you Muslim or Shiite?"

"I am a Sunni Muslim."

"What is your opinion about what is going on in Iraq after the US Army entry?"

"I heard and watched the news on the media that the Americans came to liberate Iraq. I have no political interests, and I don't have any further information."

"What about the security in your home country, the Kingdom of Saudi Arabia?"

I've travelled to many other countries in Europe, Africa, and Asia, but I did not feel more secure than in my homeland country."

"Do you belong to any religious party?"

"No, I don't."

"What do you know about Wahhabis? Do you have any connections with them?"

"I don't know anything about them."

"How do you deal with Americans in your country and how they are generally treated?"

"The American people, especially those who are in my own country, came to participate in the scientific and technological developments. For us Saudi people, we respect Americans and appreciate their efforts and sincerity. We extend the best type of treatment to them. This is based on the commands of our religion and the directions given by our rulers."

"What are the countries you have visited?"

"I visited Dubai, Kuwait, Bahrain, Egypt, Jordan, Turkey, Malaysia, Singapore, Germany, France, Holland, and Japan."

"Did you ever visit Pakistan, Iran, Afghanistan, Libya, Algeria, Sudan, or Philippines?"

"No, I never did."

"Do you have any communications with any suspicious organizations?"

"No, I do not have any association with any suspicious individuals or organizations."

"Are you an extremist?"

"Our religion is the religion of tolerance, ease, and peace. I am not an extremist."

"Do you offer your prayers and frequent *Masjids*, places of worship?"

"Yes. I maintain my five daily prescribed prayers."

"Do not you believe that five daily prayers are too much?"

"This is a religious commandment, and I follow the instructions of my faith."

"Did you travel alone while coming to the USA?"

"I was accompanied by my colleague, Engineer Mohammed AlHayyan, from Riyadh to Frankfurt."

"Who else?"

"No one else. He and I alone."

"Who is Mohammed AlHayyan?"

"He is my colleague at work. We work in the same hospital, same department, and same section."

"Since when you have known him?"

"I have known him since five years, the duration of work with him."

"What do you know about him?"

"He is a kind, intelligent, and stable gentleman."

"Does he have any feelings of extremism or political inclinations?"

"No. Never."

"How did you meet him before travelling?"

"I met him in the hospital. I parked my car there, and we drove together to the airport."

"Did you drive Mohammed AlHayyan's car?"

"No. Our colleague, Engineer Faisal AlFarisi, drove both of us in his car to the airport after we met in the hospital."

"On what day and what time was it?"

"It was yesterday evening, Friday, at eleven o'clock before midnight, local Saudi time."

"Who packed your backpack?"

"My wife did."

"Is she the one who placed those items?"

"Of course not."

"How do you know that she did not put them?"

"I have absolute confidence and trust in her. I am sure of her love to me, and she won't put in any such items."

"Then Mohammed AlHayyan put these items in your backpack."

"Of course not."

"Then you accuse Faisal AlFarisi, who drove you to the airport."

"No, I didn't say that."

"Whom do you accuse?"

"I don't accuse anyone at all. What I know is that I don't know how these items were put inside my backpack. Of course, I did not put them in personally, and I don't know who put them in. Furthermore, I don't know the nature of these items. I don't know their usage. All I know is that I passed through four inspection points in Riyadh Airport and two inspection points in Frankfurt Airport before boarding on the plane departing to Boston. My backpack was out of my sight while I was sleeping on the plane. I have no idea if any passenger opened it while I was asleep. I don't know if the backpack were opened in Logan International Airport in the secondary inspection area when the inspector ordered me to leave the backpack outside the inspection room and go into the room with him, where I stayed with him for about eight minutes."

"Do you point an accusatory finger to the customs officials or airport security officers?"

"I don't accuse anyone, but I just related to you what happened."

"What is the reason for your visit to the USA and Boston in particular?"

"I am on a training trip to be trained on a machine ordered by the hospital that I work in. I am the nominated engineer to get the training."

"Is the company's representative supposed to be waiting for you at the airport?"

"No. No one is supposed to wait for me at the airport."

"Where are planning to stay? And do you have a confirmed reservation?"

"I'll stay in Waltham, and I have a confirmed reservation."

"Now, tell me the series of events since you met your colleagues in the hospital until we met in this room."

I told him the entire story about my travel since my boss informed me about the nomination for the training trip and since I submitted my documents to the US Embassy in Riyadh. I continued the story until I arrived at Logan International Airport. He interrupted me a lot to clarify many things. His companion and the police officer interrupted me a lot as well. They had so many questions and clarifications.

I was totally exhausted. I was barely able to remember the incidents. I was trying to carefully watch what I said. I was almost stuttering. I had signed the rights list, and every word may and could be used against me in the court, even if I didn't mean it. I'd heard about people talking about the responsibility of the word. I felt and understood exactly what that meant. I comprehended the full meaning of that phrase at that time. That was almost the first time for me to converse fully in English and have a dialogue with a native English speaker for over six hours in a row.

It was a difficult time. They were tough hours. In fact, I felt the hours were like days and long, tough, and difficult periods of time. Yes, I had the right to stop the conversation at any time. But I did not have anything to hide. I did not commit any crime or sin to stop talking to them. At times, I felt that their questions were foolish and nonsense. Other times, I felt that their questions were intimidating. I was sure that their questions were mean for sure. They behaved like mean wolves.

We had honored them and treated them fairly, and we were never tough on them ever. We smiled in their faces and never frowned. We spoke to them very softly and gently. *Why are they treating us in such a mean, cruel, and ugly way? Why are they blindly oppressing us? Why they are treating me with such cruelty?* They added more questions to include more new supplementary accusations. They wanted to smear the reputation of my beloved homeland country, one well known for its widely recognized reputation in terms of nobility, generosity, and else.

Let the entire world know and learn the American justice. Let the rest of the word learn about the top human treatment and behavior throughout the ages. Let the rest of the world see how these people were treating a peaceful, unarmed person whose crime was traveling to their country seeking advancement in scientific knowledge and training in his field. I think that the moral system in the United States is biased and confused. I believe the truth and concepts had changed. I believe the wolf was wearing the leather of the innocent baby lamb.

May God the Almighty shower His mercy unto the renowned leader Saladin, the Ayyoubite. When the Crusader's army leader felt ill while in the battlefield, Saladin sent him his private medical doctor to look after him and treat him. Where are you from such ethics? Where are you from such an elite behavior in treatment?. This is our civilization. It is not your falsified civilization. There is such a great distance between the two civilizations, like that between the earth and the stars.

I completed the narration of my full story to the FBI investigators and state police officers at 9:30 p.m. I pressured myself to look fine and capable of carrying on. But the fatigue truly had overtaken me. I was shuffling and too cold. Every bone in my body was cold and aching. I was patiently waiting for this end. I could not take any further sufferings. I had said everything I knew. I'd said everything that was related or unrelated to the subject. I was hoping I would hear something that comforted me, pleased me, or even made it easy for me. I hoped for alleviation for my worries, concerns, and pains.

The FBI investigator asked again, "Should we bring you something to eat or drink?"

"No. I don't feel like eating or drinking anything."

"Do you know that the material we found in your backpack is a pyrotechnical device?"

I heard what he said, but I did not realize then that this compound was a mix of inflammable materials along with phosphoric salts that are explosive. I shook my head, and I did not even ask him what the name of the material meant. I did not even want to know the dimensions of the word. I was just hoping that I would be released or deported to my homeland.

But he carried on. "Essam. You are accused with two charges. First, you carried explosive materials on the plane. Second, you had intentionally given wrong information to the customs officer. Essam, you are under arrest."

He announced this statement, and the little faint hope I had in my mind had been fully extinguished. All the clouds of sadness and sorrow were accumulated in my life.

His words came to me like bullets. They were violent and loud like a thunderbolt. Due to the sudden and severe event, I felt fixed in place. I was overwhelmed with a deep sorrow and pain. His words made a grand earthquake in the depth of my heart, soul, and entire entity. I put my head down, thinking about my destiny. *What shall I encounter in this place where I am a stranger? I believe it is the fate and predestiny of God the Almighty. There is no escape.*

I realized the clear truth. It was as clear as the sun in the midday. All these long investigations and interrogation hours, along with so many questions, were not to seek the truth or understand the events and circumstances. Rather, it was to impose accusations, plot plights, falsify the truth, misguide people, and play on words and phrases in order to be utilized against me in the corridors of their courts. I wished they wouldn't achieve their goals. I knew for sure that God the Almighty was aware of all their plots and plans. I never expected to be arrested. Why? Where to? How?

All these questions and more crossed my mind. My head was spinning after twenty-five hours of travelling, investigation, interrogation, and all types of pressures I was exposed to for the first time in my life. I had never been exposed to being arrested, detained, imprisoned, or else, let alone being arrested outside my own homeland country. I did not even know for sure the true or real reason for arresting me. I knew for sure that it was an ambush or trap that was set up for me at Logan International Airport in Boston.

Saturday's Bleak Events Roll

When the FBI agent listed the accusations to a peaceful person like me and followed that with the arrest order, I felt that every minute item in my existence was shaken. A burning fire swept my heart and burned it. I felt that my heart was baked badly. The state police officer from Massachusetts placed the handcuffs on my wrists. He walked me through the back doors to the open backyards of the airport.

It was totally dark. The weather was extremely cold. Rainy clouds surrounded the horizon of the city from everywhere. The police squad car went through the airport's squares that had a large number of parked planes. He drove outside the airport. It was raining heavily in the city of Boston. The streets were almost dead quiet. The cars' lights were dim and surrounded with shades of fog.

Almost the entire city was totally quiet. I watched the streets while sitting in the police squad car. I did not know where we were heading. I felt overwhelmed with what was going on. I could not tell whether what was happening to me was a reality or nightmare. The police car stopped in front of a building that I could not tell what it was. It was dark and raining. The heavy pouring rain did not allow me to see clearly.

The police officer talked to the guard of the building. The guard opened the gate, and the car went inside the building. The gate was locked after we passed through. The officer parked the car in the specified parking and got out of the car. The officer, along with the two FBI investigators, asked me to walk with them while my hands were in the handcuffs.

I went inside the building. A photo was taken for me for the first time, and they took my fingerprints for both hands. I was wearing blue jeans and a blue shirt. I had a coat to protect me against the cold of this snowy city. The police officer ordered me to take off my shoes. I was only allowed to take along my Glorious Quran with me.

I was placed in a cell that was no larger than three square meters. The light in the cell was dim yellow. A camera was mounted on the inside wall of the cell for monitoring purposes. There was a toilet and water faucet. There was also a wooden seat fixed on the wall that one could barely sit on. The door of the cell was locked. What a critical moment.

I began losing feeling about time. I sat on the wooden seat while in a state of shock and confusion. I did not know what to do. My brain almost stopped functioning. I lost touch with the outside world. I tried to gather myself. I looked down at the floor of the cell. For the first time, I wept very badly. I was sobbing. I felt dizzy. The long trip, investigations, and interrogation sessions I went through were enough to make me feel sad and brokenhearted. I leaned my head on the cell's wall and felt I was out of this world for a short period. I did not know how long it took me to wake up.

I was sure that it was after midnight. I heard a noise under the door. I opened my eyes to see the jail warden placing a meal from under the door of the cell. The meal consisted of meat and a soft drink. I did not touch the meal. I did not feel like eating anything, even though I felt very hungry. I was just concerned and worried about the end of this drama. How would this catastrophe end?

In one of the darkest nights ...
While the full-moon took a nap ...
While clouds overpowered the weary star ...
A buried sigh moved strongly in my chest ...
And pain and sorrows passed through my inner self ...

I started to weep while surrounded by the darkness ...
Depression increased my pains ...
I felt an awesome Presence of the Almighty out of fear of Him ...
Truly, submitting oneself to anyone else is Blameworthy.[4]

I closed my eyes again and slept for a period of time that I did not know how long it was. It was perhaps an hour, two, three hours less, or even more. The world of time was impossible to feel in that place. When I opened my eyes again, I felt the reality of what I was suffering. It was a real world and not an imaginary one. It was a realism that I suffered. I surrendered my affairs to the Almighty Lord.

I got up from the place where I was sitting. I performed my ablution wash up for Islamic prayer. Then I returned to the wooden seat. I opened my Glorious Quran and started reading the verses of the One Most Merciful God. I felt peace and tranquility pour into my heart. I went on reciting the verses and chapters of the Glorious Quran. I did not keep track of time of my recitation. I had an inner feeling that it was due time for the *Fajr*, dawn prayer. I could not determine the source of such feeling. I stood up in the cell and offered my *Fajr* prayer.

After completing the prayer, I raised my hands to the Almighty God. I offered supplications, invocations, and tears and submitted all my requests to Him.

Oh God! To Thee I raise all of my complaints. Oh God! I am weak. Oh God! I am unable to do anything about the situation that I am in. Oh God! To You I submit my complaint about the lack of respect and humiliation that I am suffering. Oh God! You are the [True] Lord of all be-weakened people. Oh God! You are my true Lord. Oh God! To whom do You entrust me? Do You entrust me to distantly remote people who don't care for me? Or, do You entrust me to an enemy of mine whom You have granted him authority

---

[4]   A free translation of a poem written by the poet Mohammed Tawfik

over my affairs? Oh God! If You are not angry with me, I won't care [about anything]. Oh God! Your Pardon is much greater than Your wrath. Oh God! I seek refuge with the Light of Your [beautiful] Face to Whom the darkness were lit by it, and the affairs of both worlds were reformed by it, not to be worthy of Your Wrath and Anger. Oh God! To You belongs all forgiveness and pardon seeking until You are happy and satisfied. There is neither might nor power except with You.[5]

In the city of Riyadh is my dwelling home, that is, residence. In the city of Makkah dwells my heart and soul. But my fatigued body was shattered physically and spiritually here in Boston.

> *Oh My Lord! You can see my tears over my cheeks!*
> *Oh God! You can see me suffering this night alone!*[6]

It was a very lengthy and difficult night. It was a boring, depressing, and lonesome night. I felt the minutes and seconds as eternity. The passing of time was so painful to me. The gate of the cell was opened after some time. A warden ordered me to walk with him. Again, I met the two FBI agents in one of the rooms of the jail. They were the ones I met yesterday at Logan International Airport. They ordered me to sit down.

One said, "We came today to assist you. Your cooperation would help you a lot."

I replied firmly, "I told you all what I know. I answered all your questions yesterday. I have nothing to add. I would repeat exactly what you heard yesterday. Please, don't think that I am going to change my statements."

---

[5] An invocation that God's Messenger PBUH offered upon returning from the city of Taief after being subjected to severe harms of its people

[6] A free translation of a poem written by the poet Mohammed Hasan 'Awwad

They exchanged looks amongst each other, got up, and went to the next room.

A reflecting glass was in the room. They could see me, but I could not see them. A few minutes later, one of the two agents came toward me, carrying my mobile phone in his hand. They ordered me to give them a list of names stored on my mobile. I translated the contents of the contacts to English and gave it to them.

One of the agents sat down to write my statements while the other went on staring in my face, as if he were trying to read and interpret my facial features. After they had emptied the entire questions they had, I declared my desire to have an attorney to discuss my case with him. One of the agents told me that tomorrow was Monday and I should have a hearing in John Joseph Moakley Courthouse. I could ask for an attorney for the defendant. I was returned to the cell. I praised the Almighty Lord for the stability and cohesion He blessed me with.

It was 10:00 a.m. on Sunday. I was extremely happy merely to know the time at that moment. I realized that time was a grace I was deprived of. I could only know then why God the Almighty took an oath by the time. In fact, God revealed a complete Surah, a chapter in the Glorious Quran, addressing the meaning of time due to the immense importance of time in the lives of humans. Time means order and productivity. It means days, months, and years through which tasks are set and executed. A life without time is like a body without soul.

The warden handed me a breakfast meal, but I rejected it, the same I did with the lunch and dinner meals. I spent the time thinking and meditating about what was going to happen to me.

The dawn of Monday was up. I was taken out of the cell. They took me to the court. I put on my coat and shoes. They placed the handcuffs on my hands again. They ordered me to ride in the police squad car. It was snowing. A white coat of snow covered the city. I did not see the sun rising on that day. The clouds had hidden the sun completely. Every now and then, the sun faintly appeared shyly through the thick, accumulated clouds.

I looked through the city. Though it was very cold weather, people still carried on their full activities lively. All types of vehicles and pedestrians crowded the roads. I noticed people opening their stores, while others were rushing to schools. And still others were trying to get on the bus and so forth. What a busy life. I noticed people moving freely wherever they wanted. How beautiful is freedom. How ugly is oppression in a country that heads the list of defending freedoms and slaughters the humanity with the so-called freedom's dagger or knife.

Somebody allegedly and purportedly claimed that he or she is the freedom protector. They set up a statue and called it the Statue of Liberty. I think that, if that statue were able to speak, it would surely say, "Stop mocking people. Stop claiming slogans. Your reality speaks opposite to what you repeat."

The police officers were sipping their hot coffee and exchanging talks. The clock in the police squad car said 7:20 a.m. It looked like we were getting close to the courthouse. It was a very large building. The gate was large enough to allow the police squad car to pass easily. The officer headed to the back gate of the building. The sign said "Only Official Cars Are Allowed."

The police car came to a complete stop. The garage gate was closed. The two police officers left their car and placed their weapons inside special lockers in the garage. Police officers are not allowed by rules to keep on their weapons when they enter the building. One of the officers pushed the intercom button.

After few moments, the gate was opened. The officer ordered me to get out of the car after a ring of guards surrounded me, as if I were a serious criminal person. I walked with the officers inside the court. They led me to a room that was close to the garage's gate. The room was a security office for the court. They confirmed my identity and lifted my fingerprints. Before taking me to a booking area, I declared my desire to have an attorney to undertake my case.

I was led to a booking unit, which had a large number of booked people. I was booked in a case that they were the opponent as well as the judges at the same time. When the time was about 11:30 a.m., the officers ordered me to walk with steel shackles on my feet.

I was burning with sighs and sorrows. I was overwhelmed with tears that were suffocating me. I felt that the floor was barely carrying me. The officer led me to a room that was no more than one square meter only. He announced through a wall-mounted intercom that the defendant was in room number one. He left the room and locked the door. A glass window and steel net were in front of me. One could barely see through that window and steel net. There were some holes in the glass window for conversation purposes.

A rather short Caucasian woman in her upper fifties with dark black hair entered the tiny room. She was smiling. She took off her coat and sat on a seat in front of her.

She placed her purse on the table in front of her and looked at her watch. "Good morning. I am the attorney in the federal defense office who would defend you."

"Thank you very much."

"I read a bit on your case through the documents presented to me from the prosecutor. Would you explain to me briefly what happened?"

I started talking to her with my quavering voice and very cold extremities. I told her what happened with me.

As soon as I finished, the attorney surprised me by saying very confidently, "I believe you."

I was amazed. "Would you please repeat what you just said?"

"I believe you, Mr. Engineer."

"All the people I met before you did not believe that I do not know anything about those samples. Everyone before you insisted I tell him or her the truth. I don't know what the truth is that they want me to tell them."

She looked at her watch. "I'll see you in the courtroom."

"See you."

The American female attorney was truthful and daring to voice her opinion. To hell with you depressing falsifiers. To hell with you who impose injustice to others. To hell with you who have hatred against others. Here was this honest attorney declaring her truthful testimony. She uncovered the plights of the mean, unfair, and oppressing system, one that often wears the skin of a peaceful and weak baby lamb. It always pretends that it is a loyal and trustworthy advisor while hiding beneath that skin, the evils of the wolves. How often such system placed a mask over its ugly face to demonstrate civilization and advancement by carrying falsified logos of equality, justice, and freedom. To hell to those who threw me in their jails after arranging this false accusations and conspiracy. What had I committed? What had I done? What sin had I committed? I had been taken by surprise.

The attorney revealed the true and shining example of a pure and kind human being. She uncovered the game of the American system that gambles with the lives of the human being and people at large. This system hides its bad and evil intentions. It wishes to apply inhumane treatment to others.

I give many thanks to that female attorney. My faith teaches me to say to the person who did a good job, "You have done a great job." And vice versa, I would say to the person who committed an evil act, "You have done an evil act." The reward of doing a good deed is good. The punishment of doing evil is to decline such a doer and degrade him or her whenever he or she does it.

It is easy for a system that eradicated the red Indians and obliterated their identities; dropped nuclear bombs on Japan, killing hundreds of thousands; and displaced and destroyed their buildings, causing thousands of orphans. It is easy for such a system to throw a person like me in jail by a fabricated accusation and well-knit plight. I wish I could write a letter to the president of the United States saying,

Mr. President. I was—and I continue to be— confused about this issue. Therefore, I wanted to share this with you. I want to ask you about some word definitions in your dictionary, some titles, and some logos I heard from you and about you. Mr. President, what does the word "injustice" mean? What does the word "truth" mean? What do the logos of equality, justice, and freedom mean? On what your civilization is erected? What do the words "conniving," "cunning," and "devious" mean? What do the words "humiliation" and "abusing the dignity and humanity of the human beings" mean? What does "humiliation" and "humiliating" mean? What does the word "tyranny" mean? What does the words "aggression" and "violation" mean? There are many other terms that I can't list them all, and I feel insulted if I even write them. I don't want to hurt the feelings of the kind American nation by stating or writing them. Mr. President, I don't think you have the answers to my questions. But one day, you would be stopped to be asked alone about them. Be prepared. Prepare a good answer to every question. Your answer must be right. Diplomacy would not benefit you then.

While I was drowning in my imagination, writing the president's letter, someone came and took me back to the previous booking unit. It was unexpectedly warm. The temperature, as the attorney told me, was below zero Fahrenheit. The attorney noticed I was shivering of cold. A warden came to me after a few minutes and ordered me to follow him. Both my hands and feet were in cuffs and shackles. Another security officer accompanied both of us.

We went to the lift. The officer called another party through a walkie-talkie device placed on his side. He requested permission to take me to the court hall on the upper floor. Even the life was equipped in a manner that could keep prisoners on one side separately. The lift stopped at the requested floor. Before entering the courtroom, my feet were released from the shackles.

The officers took me to the defense counter. (A small plate indicated the name.) The assigned attorney lady I met was waiting for me there. We exchanged greetings. The courtroom was elegantly furnished. It had a magnificent wooden décor. The courtroom looked highly elegant. In front of us was another desk where a blonde lady, the judge's secretary, sat.

Next to us sat the prosecutor. There was an elevated counter for the witness stand. The judge's bench was higher than all other counters and stands. The judge oversees everything in the courtroom. Behind us were many seats for people who attend the court session. I could not identify any one of them. When everyone took his or her position and seat, the judge's secretary asked the defendant's attorney and prosecutor if they were ready to begin or not. She informed them that the judge would be there in few minutes.

The magistrate judge, a Caucasian with reddish facial features, entered the courtroom. Clean-shaven, he was of average height with brownish hair and a large build. He had a pair of spectacle eyeglasses on his eyes. He wore a black robe over his suit, the judge's popular gown that I always saw in movies. In fact, I had seen a judge wearing this gown while watching the movie while on the plane from Frankfurt to Boston leg of the flight. The attorney indicated for me to stand up when the judge entered the room.

After the judge sat down on his chair, his secretary said, "We are here to look into case number PBS-041004 raised by the government of the United States of America against Mr. Essam Mohammed AlMohandis. I request both parties to introduce themselves."

"I am representing Mr. Essam Mohammed AlMohandis to defend him in this case."

"I am the representative of the United States of America in this case."

The magistrate judge directed his speech toward the defense counter. "The prosecutor accuses you with two accusations. First, carrying explosive materials on the plane. Second, offering wrong information intentionally. Do you admit your guilt?"

"No, Your Honor, I am not guilty."

"Can you financially afford the expenses of an attorney?"

After discussing this matter with the attorney for a few minutes, I said, "I request the court to bear the expenses of this case."

Falsified Witness

The hearing of the case began. The government representative, the prosecutor, called upon the evidence witness and began questioning him.

"Would you introduce yourself?"

"I am the executive customs official. I've worked in this position for over twenty years. I am in charge of encountering terrorism committee in the FBI office of Boston."

"Did you hear the name of Essam Almohandis?"

"Yes. I heard it."

"When was the first time you heard about him?"

"On the third of January 2004."

"Could you tell the judge, jury, and respected listeners what you do know about Essam Almohandis?"

"I received a phone call while I was at home, and the caller told me that Essam Almohandis was being interrogated about items seized with him while being inspected in the customs area at Logan International Airport after leaving the plane on flight number four twenty-two coming from Frankfurt, Germany, which was initiated from Riyadh."

The FBI officer related the story that he heard from the customs official and a group of other officials. This was the first time I met him personally. I never saw him except in the courtroom on that day for the first time. He related a complete story and defended it very enthusiastically. He poured very strong accusations to me as if he were there and saw me at the airport, though he was seeing me for the first time and he based his testimony on a hearsay only.

My attorney asked him, "Had you seen the samples with your own eyes?"

The attorney lifted in her hand a piece of chalk that looked like one of the samples. He wasn't able to reply. He did not see anything in his own eyes. How would a person give a testimony though he did not see anything?

Many questions were given, and many gloomy and ambiguous answers were provided as well. The time set for a hearing was up. A new hearing session was set for Wednesday, January 7, 2004, at 2:00 p.m. to continue the hearing of the details of this case. The security officers escorted me to the same place I was brought from.

My goodness! What a hearing it was. There were loud voices, intensity, argumentation, and difference of opinion. I could not understand the dimensions of all what happened inside the courtroom. While in this confused state of mind, the security officer called my name. The attorney wanted to see me. I went along with him to a room, and he closed the door behind him when he left the room. The honorable attorney sat in the chair and sighed.

"I am very upset with what had happened. Ms. Conrad, what I had seen in the courtroom could only be seen in movie hall theaters."

The attorney smiled and pulled out a big volume of her briefcase. She flipped through the pages of the book. "The prosecutor accused you with two charges. First, carrying explosives on the plane. The penalty for this is between twelve to fourteen months of imprisonment. Second, giving wrong information intentionally. The penalty for this charge is five months of imprisonment. The total imprisonment is between ten to fourteen months since you did not commit any illegal things before. This, of course, if the penalties were not combined and each charge were counted and dealt with alone. But if the persecutor agreed to combine the two charges together, the total imprisonment would be zero to six months with the stop execution of the issued judgment. And then you can return home."

"What! I am on a business trip for nine days. I need to report to work after that. Failing to report to work may cause me to lose my job or jeopardize it."

"I shall do my best. I'll take care of calling your supervisors and inform them about what happened to you."

This information was severe sad news to me.

The meeting with the attorney ended. I was returned to the cell. It was almost 3:30 p.m. I did not know that I had to wait until all other inmates brought to the court had to finish their court sessions. When it was about 6:00 p.m., all the other inmates wearing the orange color prison uniform, along with me, were taken back in shackles. I remembered the Guantanamo prisoners. We were taken in a large van. I didn't know where we were taken. I didn't know my destiny. I walked alone aimlessly with broken steps.

Even my breath shook me … and even my turns around scared me!
I was like a fugitive who did not know where to go or how?[7]

I released hidden sighs and strong and urgent complaints to God the Almighty. The van driver drove us down the highway. The trip took forty minutes.

At 7:00 p.m., the van slowed down at the gate of Plymouth Correctional County Jail. The van was given permission to enter the parking area. Snow covered the ground. I was barely able to see through a small peephole in the window. The driver opened the back door of the van when he came to a complete stop. We got out of the van and entered the building. It was grey everywhere and every direction one looked. The passages of the building were narrow.

They released our shackles in the reception area. Every two prisoners were chained together from the waists for security reasons.

---

[7]   A poem for Kamel AlShannawee

We were let into a larger hall. The handcuffs and leg shackles were still on. We waited there for some time. There was a wall clock behind me, a TV set, and offices for the prison officers and wardens.

After some time, our handcuffs and feet shackles were removed. We were given orange color uniforms: a shirt, pants, and a pair of sneakers. They handed us bathroom slippers, a light blanket and cover, a toothbrush, and a tube of toothpaste with a little amount that was not sufficient to brush a child's teeth. They also passed two pieces of soap, a plastic cup, two towels, and a couple things of toilet papers.

Deep in my heart, I laughed painfully. I believe the entire rivers of the world would not be sufficient to clean the bitterness I felt. I was ordered to go to a nearby changing room and take all my street attire as well as my underwear. There was no respect, none whatsoever, to human rights or moralities. Such words look strange in the dictionaries of this place.

I passed through the humiliating inspection. I went to the hall to wait for the completion of the registration process. When my turn was up, they issued me an identification card that carried my name, date of birth, and booking number. They lifted the fingerprints of both of my hands through the scanner that was connected to the computer. The warden ordered me to stay in the same place until my cell was ready.

Everything around us was depressing. The faces of the officers and wardens did not know how to smile. But they knew well how to mock others. The walls were reinforced with concrete. Almost everything was made of concrete in this building. Everything was depressing like the depressing place itself. The colors brought the same depression, if not more. The doors were heavy steel. There were no windows. There were no plants ever. I sat on a steel seat. The seat itself complained about being cold. I was shivering. I watched the TV set in front of me. Other people like me were waiting for their unknown fate.

I didn't know how my cell would be. I didn't know who would share the same cell with me and be my companion inmate. The warden distributed a pie, an apple, and box of juice for dinner. An inmate had eaten his pie so quickly that he looked at me in a questioning manner, and then he asked if I would eat my pie or save it for later. I understood his hint. I offered him my pie and the juice, and I kept the apple to eat later. This apple would be the first meal I would eat since my foot landed in this country.

The 8:00 p.m. news bulletin started. The anchorman who was reading the news mentioned, "Saudi engineer Essam Mohammed AlMohandis appeared today before John Joseph Moakley Courthouse. He is accused of carrying explosive materials on the plane on the flight arriving from Frankfurt to Logan International Airport and intentionally giving misleading information to the customs officer."

All the people who were in the lobby, along with me, heard the news. I was shocked and appalled of what I heard. I could not believe that my name and the event were on the news. I believe it is a part of the falsified ploy.

The wardens and security people hinted and pointed to me so everyone in the hall knew who I was.

One commented, "You have a hell of a day."

Another said, "Hell with you. You have ruined your future."

Another said, "Death is better for you than staying alive."

Everyone was mocking and laughing at me.

One security officer looked very angrily at me. He screamed at me, "Get up!"

He took me away yelling, screaming, and threatening. He pushed me inside a cell and locked the door behind me. I stayed in the cell, and I was unaware of the reason for his anger. I didn't even know the reason for arresting me except what I had heard and seen.

Twenty minutes later, another security officer opened the door and ordered me to take off the orange shirt and pants. I tried to understand why they were treating me in that manner and why they were being cruel to me, but I couldn't.

One officer said, "Listen. You only obey the orders here. Execute the orders, and don't argue. I order you to take off your clothes now. Don't push me to use force with you."

Under these threatening orders and comments and due to the noted physical differences between them and me, I took off my clothes and remained with the underwear only. I was placed in a very icy cold cel I waited for a long time.

I stayed in the same situation from 9:00 p.m. until 6:00 a.m. Nobody cared for my sufferings. The outside temperature was twenty degrees below zero, according to the weather newscast. I gathered myself, trying to minimize the feeling of cold. I did like a porcupine does when it is threatened with a danger.

Some people peeked through the glass window of my room every now and then. When I became extremely tired and exhausted, I reached the steel door and knocked.

The warden on duty came to me and cruelly asked, "What do you need?"

"Why am I left in this manner?"

"If you want to get back your clothes and permit you to go to your assigned cell, you have to go to the bathroom. We'd like to make sure that you don't have any explosives in your intestines."

"Is this why I am left without clothes for nine hours?"

"Yes."

"No one informed me. I wish you made sure of that by using any medical equipment or x-ray machine."

Of course, he did not pay any attention to my statements. He talked to me in a tone full of hatred and self-pride. I went to the openly placed toilet. The officer ensured that his doubts were unreal. He handed me my orange jail uniform. I felt a little warm, though the weather was extremely cold. The warden placed handcuffs on my hands and shackles on my feet. I was ordered to wait until another security officer came to escort me to my cell. A number of guards witnessed the scene. One mocked me for my body shape.

Another said, "We shall exterminate the last one of you. We shall not allow anyone like you to come to this country."

I paid no attention to all that crap.

"Call Mohammed for help."

This officer meant God's Messenger PBUH. At this point, I could not bear the situation any more. I could not let anyone attack God's Messenger PBUH, and I kept quiet. People revealed their hatred openly. They removed their masks and appeared on their realities.

I replied angrily, "Yes. Mohammed's Lord will assist me pretty soon."

This evil person uncovered the reality of his evilness. His words revealed the reality they were trying to hide and conceal.

> *O Prophet of God! You are the master leader of the entire humanity. You are the guide of all mankind. You are sent as a mercy for the worlds. Any tragedy or pain after your loss is easy to take! You had said the truth, "I wonder about the affairs of a believer! All of his affairs are good for him. If a catastrophe occurs to him he would demonstrate patience, and if good occurs to him he would be grateful. This is only for a believer and no one else."*[8]

O my beloved Prophet of God, I heard a lot throughout the history about your great companions. I've also read a lot about them. They sacrificed their lives for yours. They sacrificed their parents and entire families for you. I am also a member of your nation, and I would sacrifice my life, soul, and beloved family for you. O Prophet of God, You are so dear to me. O Prophet of God, we are following your path

---

[8] This Hadith is reported by Imam Muslim.

despite what others say or do. We are on your path despite the barking of all those who bark, their acceptance or rejection, and their plots and plights. Our date is to meet you at your Grand Basin on the Day of Judgment. We wish to drink from your AlKawther Basin from your honorable and beloved hand. We wish to enjoy the honor and pride that God offers to those who follow you. We wish to be accompanying you in paradise. May God's peace and blessings be unto you. You are the guidance flag. May God the Almighty grant you peace as long as birds fly and the day and night rotate. May the best of peace of blessings of God the Almighty be unto you and your honorable and blessed companions forever.

The officer looked spacey. He did not know what he wanted to do with me. He went and brought another security officer. The latter addressed me kindly and politely, as if he were apologizing for the behavior of his colleague who was rough and harsh to me.

"Are you still here? No one came to take you to your assigned cell?"

He called the unit I would be placed in, as he told me. A few minutes later, another assigned security officer came and escorted me through a long passageway corridor, carrying my stuff while my feet and hands were still in steel cuffs and shackles.

"What had you done to be placed in the special criminals' cell?"

"I don't know."

"They placed you in an isolated cell alone in order not to harm anyone else. You would be under continuous monitoring of cameras. You are dangerous."

"My attorney advised me not and never to talk with anyone about my case."

The prisoner man was upset with my answer. He was more upset because of silence. Thus, he commanded me to walk quickly. The corridor was too long. My feet were in shackles. I could not walk faster than my normal pace. We passed by a basketball court, a swimming pool, a lecture hall, a computer training lab, and a reading hall. I could not believe seeing all such facilities. I finally arrived at Unit C, the northern side. A large, grey steel gate was opened.

We walked toward unit 110. Everyone in the other neighboring units looked at me. The floor was designed in two stories, an upper and lower floor. Every floor had ten units. Each unit was designed to accommodate two inmates. The area of the cell was no more than two and a half square meters. It had a toilet and two beds made of steel sheets. Both beds were fixed on the wall above each other. The bottom unit area, where I stayed, was approximately 150 square meters.

On one side was a telephone mounted on the wall. I entered my unit. I was extremely tired and hungry and feeling depressed. I wanted to throw my body on the steel bed, even if it were uncomfortable. I placed the mattress cover on it, placed the silly pillow on the mattress, and covered my body with the very light and thin cover. I was pretty cold.

I performed my ablution and offered my prayers. I wept deeply for a long time. I offered lots of prayers, supplications, and invocations to God the Almighty, who knows my place and hears my prayers and silent conversations.

I looked through a window that looked over the external space of the jail. Snow was still falling, covering the ground with a pretty white cover. I went back to my bed and tried to go to sleep. It was not long before someone opened the door of the cell and the warden ordered me to gather my given belongings and go along with him.

I hoped that there was some good news to release me. He ordered me to move to another neighboring cell until they fixed a monitoring camera on the wall that worked around the clock. I picked up my given belongings and went with him to the new place. It was too cold. My body could no longer take the situation. I suffered from severe hunger. I lost the sense of time. I was still able to differentiate between the daylight and night hours. The warden put me in unit 110 until the maintenance team mounted a monitoring camera.

It took a long time until I accompanied the warden back to the cell. The unit's head wanted to talk to me. He left me in my handcuffs and feet shackles. The system there dictated that a prisoner must not walk from one place to another unless he was in handcuffs. I had read this instructions in the office of the person in charge of the unit.

The unit head asked me about my name, nationality, and country. When he wanted to go on in his questioning, I declared the desire of myself not to talk to anyone about my case. He was very upset. He commanded the warden to put me in the cell. The warden took me to the previous cell until the monitoring camera was mounted.

They distributed the lunch meal, a piece of bread, some rice, and vegetables with meat. I was extremely hungry. I ate the rice and apple I had kept from the previous meal when I first arrived to jail. I returned the rest of the meal untouched. Another security officer came to take me to the prison's female doctor. She measured my blood pressure and body temperature.

"How much is your weight? How tall are you? Do you suffer from any diseases?"

"I am approximately seventy-four kilograms, and I am one hundred and ninety-three centimeters. I don't have any health issues. All praise is due to God the Almighty."

"Do you take any medicine on a regular basis?"

"No."

"Do you have allergy of any medicine?"

"No. I don't know of any."

"Do you drink liquors? Do you take any drugs?"

"No. All thanks are due to God the Almighty."

"Why not?"

"I am a Muslim. My faith forbids me to take anything like that."

Hesitantly, she asked,

"What brought a young man like you to this place? You have a good income. You have a family. You have a good position.

"When she noticed my lack of answers, she said something that comforted me.

"No one except me hears what you say. I am a medical doctor and a human being."

I told her in a very brief way what happened to me.

She sighed. "It looks like we are losing freedom by and by here in the USA. I don't know what the future would bring us. I wish you a better luck, Engineer."

What might I say as an unfairly treated, imprisoned person? They had plotted an accusation against me in a very dark night. Where is the America that a score of speakers described? How poor is that doctor? The gang of the White House directs all the affairs in contrary to all public slogans, noble wills, and desires.

The doctor expressed her admiration of my command of English. She was truly surprised that I did learn neither in the United States nor in England or Europe, but I rather studied in my own country, the Kingdom of Saudi Arabia. She further expressed her admiration of the Saudi development in all fields, as I mentioned some of that to her.

"Did you begin to hear some sounds or voices, or did you begin to talk to yourself while alone? I can dispense some medicines to help you conquer such symptoms if you like."

I sighed. "Thank you for your kind words and sympathy."

Lonesomeness, lack of doing anything and hallucination are the gateways for killing fears that enter the heart of the human being. They will continue to harm it until the human being falls under their influences and pains. He would not enjoy the happiness's of life. He would not enjoy any food or drink. He would not feel the happiness of sleep. He would suffer nightmares that scare him even when he is awake. He would suffer severe tiredness and fatigue. He would have a gloomy opinion [about everything]. The entire world around him becomes dark. He could only see and notice darkness. Wherever he heads, he feels that he going astray! He would become fully confused and the entire earth would become as tight as a small place to him![9]

A long time passed before I was taken back to the temporary unit to be picked up by the warden who told me that the cell was ready for me. As soon as I arrived at unit 110, the sun had already set. I offered my prayers. I had mixed feelings. I was concerned with my unknown destiny. I was yet hopeful. At times, I wept so hard until my tears dried out. Other times, I kept quiet, hoping for the appointment on Wednesday with my attorney and judge. At times, I looked at the window that looked at the inner surrounding yards of jail with bare trees and flying birds.

Tuesday was a very heavy and slow day. There were no activities on that day. They permitted me to walk about in the surrounding yards for an hour while my hands were in handcuffs and my feet were in shackles. I could not spend the entire allotted time for me to walk outside the cell. How could a person with shackles enjoy a walk in the open air? I tried to call my family, but I could not. I stayed alone inside my cell.

The dawn of Wednesday arrived. It was 4:00 a.m. when the warden brought the breakfast for me and informed me about the court date time. The breakfast consisted of milk, boiled egg, an apple, and two pieces of toast bread. I ate the apple and returned the rest of the items. The warden left me for few minutes and returned after a while, carrying the handcuffs and feet shackles. He let me out of the cell with steel cuffs on my wrists and ankles.

There is a special way for tying the hands with the cuffs. A little window is at the bottom of the cell's door. They unlock this small window and order the inmate to put his hands outside the cell. They place the handcuffs on them before they open the door of the cell. Then feet shackles would be placed on the feet after the door of the cell is opened and the hands are cuffed already.

---

[9]   Hamad AlJaser, *Memoires*, vol. 1.

I picked up all my given belongings and placed them in a plastic bag handed to me by the warden. I followed him to the hall. I was kept in a room there until 7:00 a.m. Every three inmates were chained together. We were subjected to a humiliating body search and inspection. By the time the external door was opened, I felt so cold that my limbs were almost frozen. I tried my best with the man in charge to let me wear my coat, but all my efforts went in vain. He refused to let me wear my coat, though I was extremely cold.

When all inmates were ready, they took us in a van to John Joseph Moakley Courthouse. It was cloudy and rainy. The road from Plymouth to Boston was overcrowded. My limbs turned blue because of the handcuffs and feet shackles. Thanks to the driver who turned on the heater in the van. Yet I was shivering cold. He crossed the highway toward Boston. I could see the roads through a peephole.

I enjoyed the scenery of the sky, landscape, buildings, road signs, cars, and crossing pedestrians. In short, I was able to see the life again. How difficult it is to live on the life's margin. One could only see grey color in the Plymouth jail. The only other color I could see was the white falling snow. I could see the snow from the window of my cell. Life is frozen in the jail. One could only hear the squeaking steel doors and unlatching and latching steel doors. One's number of breaths was counted there. One's whispers are countable, heard, and reported. There was no conversation there, but rather, orders were given, and commands were executed.

While I was still staring on what I could see on the road, the jail van driver stopped abruptly at the gate of the court. The guards let him in through the gate leading to the parking inside the spacious building. I could only see a very small portion of that grand building of the court. We were let out of the jail van one person at a time. We were let into the court building. There was a great difference in temperature between the outside and inside of the court.

Blood flew back in my limbs again. All the prisoners were placed in one cell. The security officer ordered me to walk along with him.

He opened a special cell away from the rest of the prisoners' cells. As soon as he locked the door of my cell, I realized his purpose. He wanted to place me in a single and extremely cold cell alone, away from the heated other cells.

It was almost 9:00 a.m. My appointment, as far as I could remember, was approximately 2:30 p.m. I sat alone, silently offering Remembrance of God the Almighty and meditating. I offered sincere supplications and invocations sincerely to God.

The place was totally quiet. There were no windows or any opening therein. A monitoring device protected with steel bars was fixed on the grey wall. There was a toilet in the room to answer the call of nature if need be. A steel seat added to my feelings of severe cold. I had a double feeling of pain. One was psychological; the other was physical. I expected to come down with the flu or cold at any time because of that and the weather changes. I didn't have any sufficient rest, food, or sleep. But I remembered the Arab poet who said, "If the Divine's Care took care of you … Sleep. All your fears are taken care of."[10]

How could a person who feels the togetherness and support of the Creator, God the Almighty, feel ill or humiliated, while God is with him in observation and support and backs every step of the way and in all affairs and needs?

The door of the cell was opened again. The prison officer ordered me to follow him. I walked very slowly behind him because of the shackles. The officer informed me that the attorney wanted to sit with me and talk to me. He took me to one of the rooms there, where I sat in a chair. There was a window in front of me through which I could barely see anything.

A few moments later, the lady attorney came in the room. She asked me about my situation in the jail. I related to her how badly I was treated and how badly they were humiliating me. I told her how cruel they were to me and how they tried to force me to talk about

---

[10]   Ahmad Shawqui, the prince of Arab poets

my case. I mentioned to her that I refused to say anything to them. The attorney was very upset with what was going on with me in jail. I felt that from her voice tone and facial expressions. She hated injustice, unfairness, oppression, and the cruelty they were treating me with inside the jail.

But she had no control over this. Furthermore, there was no materialistic evidence that she could use against them in such case. It sufficed me to see such feelings and sympathy from her. I felt that she had humanitarian feelings and sympathy. This feeling demonstrated to me that some aspects of the Western and human personality reject oppression and aggression on others' freedoms. I told her about the news bulletin that I heard along with the other prisoners and prison administration when they talked about me by name on the news bulletin.

She told me that the media was good enough not to publish my pictures on the newspapers and satellite channels. I asked her when I would be able to get out of jail. She told me that she would attempt before the court today under a fifty thousand-dollar bond. The sum was large, but it was only a bond until the court sessions began. They wanted to ensure my presence at court, provided the judge approved that I could go back home.

The officer returned me to the freezing cell. When the time came, we took the elevator as usual, and we walked into the courtroom. The officer released my hands and feet from cuffs and shackles before entering the courtroom. I met the attorney there, and I greeted her. She had a smile on her face. I sat with full confidence that God the Almighty would remove the hardships for me. I believe that everything is in God the Almighty's control. When both parties, the prosecutor and my attorney, were ready, the magistrate judge walked in. Each party introduced himself to look into my case.

My attorney stood up. "I received yesterday a number of letters that ensure the good character of my defendant. I received letters from his boss, colleagues, his father, brother, and some of his friends and neighbors as well."

The attorney started reading portions of those letters. She cited some of the quotes written therein. This was a pleasant surprise to me. She did not inform me about them before we came to the courtroom.

"Your Honor," she declared, "I suggest that my defendant, the Saudi engineer, be released and returned to his homeland country until we begin the proceedings of his case. May I request Your Honor to order releasing him under a fifty thousand-dollar bond?"

The prosecutor objected to her request. "Your Honor, he should not be released from jail just because testimonies about his good character and conduct that the defense attorney submitted. Neither should he be released under a bond. We need confirmed guarantees that he would attend the court sessions whenever the American government decides."

The attorney reacted to the intervention of the prosecutor. The discussion became tense. The magistrate judge ordered both sides to quiet down.

The magistrate judge announced, "I see that we should wait until the next session of the court to ensure that the suggested bond is available. The court also accepts the defense attorney's suggestion if the Saudi government guarantees the return of engineer on the proposed date for the court."

But the prosecutor had a different opinion. "Your Honor, the Immigration Services canceled the defendant's visa. He would not be able to enter the USA to attend the court sessions if he leaves now."

The magistrate judge's commented decisively. "The court can issue an order to permit the defendant to re-enter the USA for the purpose of the completion of the court's proceedings."

When the allotted time for the session ended, the magistrate judge suggested completing the discussions on Friday: January 9th, 2004. The prosecutor did not feel happy with what the magistrate judge had said.

I went to the ground floor of the court and met my attorney there.

"Were you able to speak with your family?"

"No. Unfortunately, I could not."

"Why not?"

"There are some missing paperwork procedures in the jail about that."

"It's all right. I shall talk to the people in charge in the Plymouth jail."

"I don't know how to thank you for your kind efforts."

"I want you strong. Well, good-bye for now."

"Good-bye."

This meeting ended at 3:30 p.m. Upon the time of return to jail, after all the prisoners completed their court sessions, the officers took us back to jail. The van started the return-to-jail journey. By that time, it was totally dark around Boston. I felt that my tension eased up a little. My day began at 4:00 a.m. this morning.

On my way back to my cell, I met some wardens in the jail. My case became a popular one in the jail. Both the officers and inmates were curious to know what had happened to me. Some inquired about the court session, while others cracked jokes about me. I did not pay attention to either party. I arrived at Unit C, cell number 110.

I went into a discomforting sleep after I offered my prayers.

I usually woke up on the noise of the officers who distribute the food to the inmates at about 4:00 a.m. before dawn and sunrise. I could look through the window and see some traces of the light of dawn about that time. When I see that, I stand to offer my *Fajr*, dawn prayer. The dawn of Thursday appeared, and the early rays of the sunrise were visible. The scene of the sunrise is so beautiful. I did not see the sun rising because I was placed in this jail. "There is nothing more beautiful under the sun from the sun itself."[11]

The scene of the thick branches and leafless trees carrying snow on them was also wonderful. Drops of pearls fell on the ground

---

11   Badr Shaker AlSayyab; an Iraqi poet.

like water from those thick-branched trees. I could see fresh green branches and twigs of the trees. I could also see a number of seagulls flying in the sky. It was a nice scene though it was from behind the bars of the jail's window.

One of the bounties of God the Almighty is to be able to think about the various creations of God and meditate about His oneness, greatness, omnipotence, and vast kingship. My thoughts moved toward my parents and all my family members. I thought about how they were feeling after hearing my sad news. I thought to myself for a moment without any previous planning or set appointment.

The warden came to me. "Your attorney wants to speak with you on the phone."

She told me that she had arranged with the in-charge authority in the jail to let me talk to my family over the phone. She further mentioned that she spoke to my boss at work in Saudi Arabia who expressed his vast interest to support me in every possible means, materialistically and emotionally. He requested her to express the regards of my colleagues, friends, and all those who sympathized with me of those who knew me and those who didn't know me as well. He further mentioned to her that the hospital also supported my case and me until it was solved favorably.

It was a feeling of love, togetherness, and support by all. It was a feeling of a one single body. One can't imagine how happy I was to hear that. I longed for more news of this type. It was the place where I could draw more patience and perseverance. I believe this was the grace of God the Almighty unto me before anything else.

I returned to my cell feeling the warmth all over my body, although the weather was pretty cold. I was very surprised to see some inmates wearing shorts in that place. I went on thinking about how my wife received the bad news. She was still in her few first days of afterbirth confinement. I wonder about the situation of my two little children, my son Mohammed and my little daughter Wasan.

The call of the warden in the jail interrupted me. He asked me to accompany him to the same female doctor whom I met on the first day I arrived at jail. She tested me for tuberculosis PPD by injecting a vaccine under the skin to get the result after two days. I was returned to my cell, and I waited for the sunset of Thursday and sunrise of Friday.

As it was my habit, I sat for a while. Then I went to bed. I was used to getting up at 4:00 a.m. around dawn time. I waited until I offered my prayer, and I stayed up until the evening, the time to sleep.

> *You could see me roaring at the time of battles!*
> *You could see me kneeling in the niche praying …*
> *I glorify my Great Lord while prostrating …*
> *And my supplications knock the gate of heavens!*[12]

I had greatly wished that they allowed me to have my companion Glorious Quran with me in the cell. It would keep me company and relieve my lonesomeness. I had also greatly wished they permitted me to have a pen and writing paper to write and pour my feelings that were cluttering in my chest.

The sun rose on Friday. But it did not have any rays. This day was supposed to be the last of my training session days on the medical equipment I came to Boston to train on. Sunday was supposed to be the day of return to my dear and beloved homeland. But this was the fate of God the Almighty. He does as He pleases.

The warden came to ask me if I liked to take a bath. How could I take a shower in an open place? Everyone stands naked without any bashfulness. They neither respect the Almighty God nor shy from their fellow human beings. It was 4:00 a.m. The warden handed me a container to put my given belongings, including my sleeping mat, in it.

I returned the breakfast as usual, except for the apple. The officer led me to the reception area where he placed me in a room until all

---

12   A poem of AbdulHamid AlSaqr

the prisoners who had to appear in the court gathered there. I was surprised to see the warden bringing my outfit that I wore upon arrival at the jail for the first time. I put it on quickly, hoping that this was a good omen.

After the jail officers took every necessary precautions of tightening the shackles and handcuffs on the wrists, they ordered us to ride in the van to go to John Joseph Moakley's Courthouse. The road was crowded. The weather was cold, but I felt warm wearing my own normal clothes. I felt the warmth of my own coat. The van was also warm. The van driver, along with his companion, was sipping their warm coffee. I was deprived to enjoy a hot cup of coffee for quite some time.

The prisoner next to me said, "The judge sentenced me to ten years in jail."

The prisoner sitting next to him commented, "Don't worry. I have spent three years in jail thus far. After the first three months, you get used to the place, and you feel comfortable around the people there."

Here I was, sitting with veteran prisoners with long criminal histories and dishonorable records. Each one of the prisoners went on telling the other about his adventures. I did not like their stories. I kept myself busy looking through the holes of the window that looked at the driver's chamber. I looked at the roads. The van stopped inside the court building. We were ordered to get out of the van.

For the second time, the officer purposely took me to a freezing cell alone without any reason that was explained to me. I could only see how much hatred they had and how mean they were to me. This time, I was wearing my own coat and clothes. This decreased the freezing cold of the cell they put me in.

Release Conditions and Return Home

Just a little before my appointment with the judge, I met my attorney, who gave me the glad tidings and news. She informed me that she had received a check for the amount of fifty thousand dollars in the name of the American government. My brother Yousuf had sent that check. She was also about to get a letter from the embassy of the Kingdom of Saudi Arabia, my homeland country, that ensured my presence before the court to attend the court session when it was held. I wept and thanked God the Almighty tremendously for His grace.

I was taken to the courtroom upstairs. The magistrate judge arrived at the courtroom.

My attorney stood up. "I declare before your honorable and respected court and all those who are present in this court that a treasurer check in the amount of fifty thousand dollars in the name of the American government is ready for you. Also, we are awaiting a letter from the Saudi government ensuring the presence of Mr. Essam AlMohandis before the American justice in the time specified by the court for the session."

The prosecutor objected. "Your Honor, arranging the sum in such a timely manner reflects that the sum is too little. This is done to return the accused person to his country and family. The government expects that the defendant would pay back this sum to his family and friends on installment basis, or else, they may elect to not take the sum totally. Therefore, sir—"

The defendant attorney said angrily, "My defendant has nothing against him. He has no accusation or involvement in using what was found in his backpack. He doesn't have to run away from the court. Furthermore, we did not hear the experts' opinion concerning the samples."

The voices of both the defense representing me in the case and the prosecutor that was representing the government got louder.

The prosecutor said in a crystal clear and strong voice that shook the sides of the courtroom, "Your Honor, I reviewed the rules, regulations, and government laws and found no memorandum of understanding between the two governments—the US and Saudi governments—to hand over the persons wanted for court. That is if the American government requested the accused person to be handed over to them for court purposes. The American government is of the opinion to keep the accused party in custody until a sentence is announced. We do this in support of justice and in materialization of justice as well."

The voice of the defendant attorney also became as loud. "Your Honor, I have spoken with the people in charge in the Saudi Embassy, and I am about to receive a letter ensuring the attendance of Mr. Essam AlMohandis in court whenever the court requests. Therefore, I appeal to this court to wait and not to jump too fast to conclusions."

The magistrate judge favored the defendant attorney's opinion. As for the prosecutor, he didn't like that at all. He suspected what the defendant attorney said concerning the letter from the Saudi Embassy. He tried hard, but all went in vain to go back to the issue of the value of the check that it was too little. But the magistrate judge sustained the prosecutor's statement. The judge further issued a decree to set me free based on specific conditions.

At this point, the prosecutor threatened to use his appeal to the court's decision and request to remove the case to the Supreme Court. About the end of the time allotted for this case, the magistrate judge directed both the prosecutor and defense attorney to sit together and reach a mutual agreement about this issue.

The magistrate judge ordered my release and return to my homeland based on the following conditions:

1. The defense guarantees in writing and in an open court session that the defendant returns from the Kingdom of Saudi Arabia and fully cooperates with the governments of the United States and the Saudi government on this case to appear in front of this court upon its call.

2. The defense provides a financial bond of fifty thousand dollars (US) that would be recorded in the court's records.

3. When the defendant returns to the Kingdom of Saudi Arabia, he must remain in his current address and not move to another address without a previous permission.

4. The defense will appear at the pre-appeal office before 4:00 p.m. (US time) every Wednesday of each week to coordinate with them, besides his weekly appearance at the US Embassy offices in Riyadh.

5. The defendant must deliver his passport to the US Embassy in Riyadh immediately upon his return to the Kingdom of Saudi Arabia.

6. The defendant must maintain his current position during his conditional release period.

7. The defendant must not be engaged or involved in any crimes during his conditional release period.

8. The defendant must not obtain any hand arms or other destructive weapons during his conditional release period.

9. The defendant must not travel outside the Kingdom of Saudi Arabia except for the purpose of returning to the United States to appear in court.

How Things Are Inside a Plymouth County Correctional Facility (PCCF)

The next Tuesday was set as an appointment if the prosecutor and defense attorney mutually didn't agree on the decision of the magistrate judge. The meeting was resolved in this foggy manner. How would the magistrate judge issue a decision while the prosecutor had the right to reject or appeal it?

When I met the attorney, she came to the tiny cell with another person, a young man in his twenties, with her. She introduced the man to me. She said he was her investigation assistant. She asked him for a testimony in the hearing in the court. His eyes shone with intelligence. He was very kind, active, nice, and fully sympathetic with me personally and my case.

The attorney continued to say, "The judge has no final say over the case. His position and legal authorities don't permit him to do so. The prosecutor may appeal the sentence or decision of the magistrate judge. Then the case has to be moved to the judge who has higher and absolute authorities. Maybe you would be released on Tuesday and be allowed to go back home until the time when the court is resumed. Also, maybe the case would be transferred to another judge in John Joseph Moakley."

I reminded her of my work, family members, and children. The defense attorney was fully cooperative with me, but there was no better thing that she could do.

I was returned to Plymouth County Correctional Facility (PCCF). I went through sadness and depression states. I didn't know what to do or where to go. It is awful to have a feeling of oppression and injustice done to you. What I noticed of the prosecutor to affix the accusation to me was unbearable and intolerable. He was trying very hard to keep me in jail under custody. This was truly bad, evil, and awful to me.

Upon getting into the jail and being stripped of my clothes again, I was given the jail's orange uniform. I carried the plastic container with my stuff to my cell in unit C, cell number 110. On the way to the cell, I bumped into the on-duty captain, an elderly man.

He stopped me. "What is the matter? Weren't you released? What is the matter?"

I was truly depressed and upset. I don't know what I told him at the time. I continued my way to the cell, looking down to the floor. When I reached my cell, I wept very badly. The warden locked the door after he put me inside the cell. I cried for a while. I felt so bad.

It was Friday. I remembered the time I visited my parents' home every Friday, in which my beloved wife and children accompanied me. I remembered how happy my parents felt when we visited them. I remembered how I used to wander about freely in the peaceful city of Riyadh. I remembered how lovely life was. I remembered my work, my colleagues, and all my good friends.

The appointment was too far this time. Saturday, Sunday, and Monday of the second week of my visit to the United States passed while living in a boring routine life in jail. I was allowed to walk in the jail's inner yard one hour a day, the only allowable activity I could do. It is a walk where no one is allowed to talk to you in it. I spent some time reading the papers that the attorney handed over to me after the last hearing session.

On Monday, the monitoring camera in my cell malfunctioned. The maintenance team arrived on the scene to fix it. The warden took me to cell 107, whose inmate had a court session.

Cell 107 looked at another angle of the prison. There was nothing else other than two steel bunk beds, unlike my cell with only a single bed and monitoring camera. There were no monitoring cameras in the other neighboring cells, as I learned later on. While I was in cell 107, I found two ballpoint pens. I took one of them and wrote a note to the owner.

I said in the note, "I am your neighbor in cell 110. I borrowed one of your pens, and I shall return it to you tomorrow in the walk break in the jail's inner yard."

I happily took the pen along. When I was returned to my cell after repairing the monitoring camera, I drew a table illustrating the days of the week and dates. I was afraid to lose track of time and days. The pen was designed in a special way that fulfills the jail's safety and regulation. Writing with this pen was painful to the fingers because of its special aching design.

While looking on the documents of my case, an officer came to the cell and opened the door. He ordered me to come to the office and call the attorney. I memorized her phone number by heart so as I would not be forced to turn it in for any reason. I called her.

She immediately told me, "I know you were unable to call your family."

"I miss my parents, and I am longing to hear the voices of all my family members."

"I'll connect you to talk to them right away."

"Is this true?"

"Yes. In just a few moments, you'll talk to them."

I couldn't hide my happiness to what the attorney had said. I was burning inside. I declared to her my desire to talk to my parents. I dictated their phone number. My heartbeats went up while listening to the rings of the phone on the other end. I raised my voice when the other party picked up the receiver.

"Peace be unto you."

"Peace be unto you, too, Essam."

I could not talk. I burst in tears. "Yes, Dad. This is Essam."

"How are you, Son? How is your situation now?"

"All praise is due to God the Almighty. I am fine. How are you? How is all the family?"

"Everyone here is fine. They send their greetings and regards. They are all praying for you all the time. My dear, Son, have patience and perseverance. Oppression is not but darkness. The light of truth is stunning. The darkness of the night would not stop or prevent the light of truth even if the darkness prolonged."

"All praise is due to God the Almighty. All praise is due to God the Almighty."

"Your mother, wife, children, aunts, uncles, and brothers and sisters are well, and we all miss you very much and long for seeing you back among us."

"May God the Almighty preserve your life and bless your heart, my dear dad."

"We are sure of the ease is coming from God the Almighty. I have high hopes and firm confidence."

I received the voice of my parents from thousands or tens of thousands of miles away. It was strong, firm, crisp, and assuring. They told me to be patient and have perseverance. They said that God the Almighty would take care of me and release me.

I spoke with my brother Yousef, the most beloved to me among all my brothers. He is the undeclared hero. He is the companion of my long life path. He was the coordinator, the synchronizer in this calamity. He is one of the best companions in difficult times and hardships. He coordinated the efforts between the attorney and my family.

I felt the tune of sadness in his voice, though he tried his best to hide it. It is rather one of the most difficult things to hide human emotions, especially when people know one another for a long time. How could the emotions of parents, brothers and sisters, friends, and mutual marital relationship emotions be hidden?

I was sure after this call that the news of my arrest and jail had spread all over in my hometown after a satellite station announced what it wanted to say about the incident. Some newspapers and magazines also wrote and published what they wanted to say. The word of mouth spread amongst people about the incident as well. They all didn't bother to investigate their statements. The Western media took the leading role in publishing what they wanted about it. The rest were mere followers. They competed with one another about who would publish the news about the incident first. They didn't bother about the truth, originality, and trustworthiness.

It was sad to hear my news on the media in a negative way. I believe the media profession is going downhill. The honest media is supposed to help the oppressed and stop the oppressors. Even the professional media people lives were endangered and exposed to risks. They are supposed to defend the truth. Even they paid their life as a price for that. But here we are suffering a media that leads people astray, misguides them, forges the truth, and falsely accuses people with crimes they did not commit. This media aims to harm the reputation of my country. They want to put the reputation of my country in mud out of envy and hatred. They are unhappy to see this country, the Kingdom of Saudi Arabia, committing to the laws and regulations of God the Almighty .

I felt bad to read the write-ups of some "bat or vampire" writers. Such writers write in the dark while enjoying the comfort of their comfortable chairs. Their main purpose is to shine their names on a newspaper and media without any effort to authenticate their writings. They merely support an entity with a bad content. This plan had been designed by the enemies of such great entity and blessed by those who applaud and squeak by voice or tongue of the fifth column and bats of the dark.

HRH Prince Mohammed bin Nayef bin AbdulAziz met my old father in his office, and he truly honored us by that. He supported us morally and emotionally with his kind words and support. The words of the prince to my father were a healing medicine. They were silencers for the barking dogs. This is not a strange act of HRH

Prince Mohammed. This behavior is in the genes of the royal family. They are loyal to their people. I had enough support of the words of the prince more than anything else. My brother related to me how my family received the bad news about my imprisonment.

The warden returned me to the cell. I was so happy on that day. I was happy with the news I heard from my family members, except my wife who did not know anything about me until that time.

On my way back from fresh air hour, I met the inmate in cell 107. I thanked him for the pen I borrowed from his cell while he was away in the court. He refused to take it back and told me to keep it. I was so happy to keep the pen and for the favor done by the prisoner. I hoped to jot down some ideas, comments, or anything else while alone in the cell. I thought I might remember some notes to write down and tell the attorney about them later on when I saw her. The fresh air walking break was over, and I returned back to my cell late.

I went to sleep, but it was not a deep and comforting sleep. At 4:00 a.m., as usual, an officer came to get me. He handed me a breakfast and plastic container to gather my things in it. We went to the waiting area. From there, we were taken in the jail's van to the court. My head was spinning with conflicting thoughts. *Would they release me from jail prematurely until the court's date? Would I leave today to go back to my country and meet my loved ones at home?*

I let my mind dream with imaginations. I was dreaming about freedom. I dreamt about many nice things I was deprived to do. The van stopped inside the depressing court building. The guards there treated me very cruelly. The officer in charge loved to put me in the same freezing room every time I came to the court.

I got the courage to ask the guard, "Why do you put me alone in this freezing room?"

"I just follow orders."

I praised my Lord, God the Almighty, for granting me enough patience and perseverance to withstand all those difficulties. Here I was sitting alone. I squatted in my place. I could not deliberate anything. The smell of pain and inability filled the place. There were very faint rays of hope and optimism. But I had a great hope in God who runs and manages the entire affairs of the universe.

Patty Saris, the Judge

"Keep the Suspect in Boston until the Court Date and Issuing the Sentence"

I met with the defense attorney along with her young active assistant. She told me that the prosecutor rejected the magistrate judge's order to release me while my case was still before the court. I did express my pessimism of what was going on. I wondered if the judge in charge of my case were flexible. Or did she commit to the teeth about the written laws? Did she have considerations for the humanitarian aspects or emotions? Did she look deep into the matters and read between the lines?

I arrived at the court, and the judge, a thin Caucasian woman of middle height with short hair, sat on her chair. She was wearing the traditional judge's cloak with wide black sleeves. Two young male officers accompanied the judge when she came in the courtroom. She did not care too much about the old fashion and traditional appearance of the magistrate judges. Despite my opinion about the judge, as my imaginary mind drowned it earlier, I did not feel any fear or concerns about the judge.

She announced the decision. "The suspect must be kept in custody until the date of the court. This is the opinion of the prosecutor."

The defense attorney intervened. "I would like to remind Your Honor that the court has received the sum of the bond in the

American Treasury and about to receive a letter from the Saudi government to ensure the presence of Mr. Almohandis at court in the time set by the court."

The prosecutor intervened, saying he objected that the suspect would leave and go back to his country. He insisted on my stay in the United States until the date of the court. The judge confirmed his request. My attorney requested the judge to release me from jail and put me under house arrest with electronic device monitoring system, especially there was no fear from my presence among public.

Another round of discussions, dealings, and objections took place. All praise is due to God the Almighty. This round ended in favor of my attorney, who surprised the court with a much dangerous case where the court approved a house arrest and electronic monitoring devices for the suspect.

Tuesday's hearing session ended not to the liking of the prosecutor. The judge approved the suggestion of the defense attorney through coordination with the Special Appeal Office. She issued an order to start the execution of the necessary procedures. She set the next court date hearing on Friday.

I met the attorney in the same usual room on the ground floor of the court. She said that this was a little progress in the proceeding of the case. I tried to discuss the matter with her, attempting to get further information about the chance I had to win the case, but she told me it was too early to tell and she was propose to postpone our discussion about the details for a later date.

Friday, January 23, 2004

I was returned to PCCF. It was cold. Every part of my body was freezing cold. I was more confused. I felt more assured that God the Almighty would not put me to waste. But I cried because of injustice and oppression. I cried because of treachery and backstabbing. I cried to see bright slogans up in the air, such as freedom, justice, equality, and human rights protection. And all of that is all lies, cheating, and fraud. Oh God, I longed for freedom. I hate lonesome prisons. I felt miserable about the treatment I received from the jailers. Here I was in front of the captain, an old, soft-spoken man with good manners, who met me the last time.

"Good evening, Engineer Essam. You look better than last time."

"Good evening, captain. All praise is due to God the Almighty for all His grace."

"Tell me what happened today."

"Things are positive. All praise is due."

"Good. I'm happy to hear this. Did you receive any messages from your family members?"

"No."

"Ask them to send their messages. I'll get them and deliver them to you personally."

"This is very kind of you, captain."

"Do you know that I have a son your age? He is an engineer like you, and I don't think that you are guilty. I'm sure there is a mistake."

"Thank you very much for your kind thoughts."

"My best wishes to you. Good luck, and good-bye."

"Good-bye, captain."

I felt good hearing the captain's words. I became full of enthusiasm and vitality. My strides became wider. I was truly happier. How many times can you hear words that feel like honey and others like killing poison? How many times can a word indicate to the pronouncer, "Leave me alone. Drop me. Don't utter me"? And how many times can a word bring the one who says it to a greater status?

I headed toward my cell. The words of the captain and attorney were still echoing in my ears. They were so kind and sweet. They were exactly opposite to the words and treatments of the Delete jailers and guards of the jail. I felt sad about the dedicated attempt of the prosecutor to put the handcuffs on my wrists and throw me inside the jail, trying to accuse me with a false accusation. I'm sure you remember the wolf that was accused with eating Prophet Joseph, son of Jacob. That was a crime that the wolf did not commit.

I went inside the cell and stared at the ceiling. I kept on asking myself, *How many innocent prisoners are there in the jails? How many people are thrown in jails by unjust, unfair, and oppressing hands? May such sinful hands be ruined.*

It was Wednesday evening. I was sitting on the cold, steel bed. My soul ached of the steel. My ribs ached of it, too. A brownish color person stood by the door of the cell. I thought him to be one of those who ridiculed me.

He addressed me in broken Arabic. "Peace be unto you, my brother."

I got up from my place as if a snake had bitten me. In a moment, I was holding the door of the cell. I thought to myself, *Who could come here and greet me with the Islamic greeting?* I'd been here for more than nineteen days, and no one at all greeted me in such a greeting. I did not hear such pure words for the entire time I was in this jail. I wished I could give him a big hug. Offering the greeting of peace is in itself a feeling of comfort, peace, satisfaction, and tranquility.

"Peace be unto you, too. How are you?"

"All praise is due to God the Almighty. I'm fine. How about you?"

"I'm fine, too. All praise is due to God. Be patient. Leave your affairs to God the Almighty."

"All praise is due to God the Almighty in all cases and situations."

I didn't want to stay long so we would not get harmed.

And before this man left, he asked me, "Do you have a copy of the Glorious Quran?"

"I'm terribly sorry. All of my belongings are in the prison's custody."

There were no ties between me and the man in terms of country, nationality, race, and language, but the only tie was Islam. It is the religion of peace that brings the hearts of people together. If Islam touched and reached the innermost part of the heart of a person, he would feel the peace, brotherhood, and sense of eternity with other Muslims all over the globe. God the Almighty stated in the Glorious Quran, Aal-Imran the Family of Imran 3:103, "By His Grace you became brothers."

We shook hands with our hearts and were unable to touch the hand of one another. We exchanged words, though we did not to open our mouths with one word to one another. The surprise was when he came back again to me. He handed me the Glorious Quran from underneath the door. He requested me to take care of it and preserve it. He asked me to return it to him when I finished my reading.

I got the copy of the Glorious Quran and thanked him tremendously for it and his favor. I asked God the Almighty to release him from jail and set him free again. I began reciting the verses of the Glorious Quran. The only time I stopped was the due time for the prayers and time for sleep. That night was the most pleasant night for me as the Glorious Quran was my companion in jail.

On Thursday morning, I passed by the Muslim brother in cell 108 while going for a walk in the inner jail's yard. I had been in the same jail for over nineteen days, and he and I never met personally. Only one cell separated him from me.

He mentioned to me that he knew about my case and he knew the prosecutor who was in charge of my case. He mentioned that this prosecutor was known for being tough, cruel, strict, and harsh on people. He wished me luck in my case. He mentioned to me that I could request a copy of the Glorious Quran and other books from the jail administration if I desired to do so. He also mentioned to me that I could request the visit of the *Masjids* of the Boston imam when he came to pay a visit to the inmates in the jail, though this imam was currently on a trip outside the United States. He also noticed that I refused to eat the food and I turned it back every time they brought it to me. He, along with his cellmate, asked me to take care of my health and leave my situation to the Almighty God, as He was the best caretaker.

The night approached, and Friday dawn appeared. I was fully hopeful that God the Almighty would make a way out for me from this mess and jail. I wished to go back home, see my family members, and be at home. I left the prison to go to the court. I placed the copy of the Glorious Quran under the cell's door of my comrade in cell 108, as we had agreed. I could not say good-bye to him, as he was still asleep and it was too early for him to wake up.

I put on my clothes, and we headed toward the court. When my turn to appear in court came, I noticed a number of people sitting in the back that I didn't know. Among this group of people was my attorney's assistant. The judge and her secretary entered the courtroom.

My attorney stood up and surprised me and the court that she found a place that fulfilled the preconditions set by the court's coordination office. She didn't inform me about this while meeting with her before we went upstairs to the courtroom. All concerned parties agreed on the time to begin the hearings for my case. It was set for one month from that date. The defense attorney accepted, provided she would be fully prepared for the hearings. Otherwise, she would ask for postponement for another month.

I was taken by the elevator to the cell downstairs. This time, the officer didn't put me in the freezing cell, but he put me in a large room with many other prisoners. After a long waiting period where my attorney completed the required paperwork to release me from jail and put me under house arrest and electronic monitoring, the officer ordered me to follow him. That was at noon.

The officer released the feet shackles, and he released my handcuffs this time and ordered me to follow him. I walked behind him in a long corridor. I reached a big gateway. At the gateway, the attorney and her young assistant were waiting for me. I froze for a moment in my place. I felt the blood was running again in my body. But my eyes refused but to look around and discover this new place. I could not believe that I was free again.

I felt a tremendous happiness, but it was a silent contentment. I could not believe that I had no handcuffs or feet shackles and I was set free. *Am I going to stop hearing the squeaks of the cells' doors in the prison? Is the ill treatment of the jail's officers going to end? Is the poor treatment of the prison's guards going to end? Is the verbal and physical humiliation of the jail's officers and ward guards going to end?*

I ran toward the attorney and her assistant, and they ran toward me as well. The white snow scattered in every direction as a result of our footprints. I was taken by surprise with this news. I hugged the attorney's assistant with excitement and happiness giggles. Joy and happiness overwhelmed me. I greeted the respected and honorable lady, the attorney. The joy was noticed all over her facial features.

Everything around me became pretty. The sun was shining. The birds were flying up in the air. The sound of the waves in the ocean was attractive. The color of the blue sky was beautiful. Even the cold air touching my cheeks was lovely. It was like everything came together to greet me for being out of jail. All praise is due to You, God the Almighty.

I put on my hat and gloves to protect myself against the cold wind. We headed toward the follow-up cases office. I received my backpack with all my personal items. I got back my money that I brought to the United States with me. They kept my passport and my return tickets. They took more photos of me, and I signed some documents in order to commit to the release conditions. Otherwise, they would apply additional penalties.

The attorney reviewed the documents, read release the conditions, and asked me to sign the documents so I could be released from jail. I couldn't believe my eyes. The court building is a beautiful architecture design constructed of wonderful red stones facing the ocean. Beautiful marbles cover its floors. I couldn't imagine while I was inside the court that the other face of the court's building is as pretty and has lovely colors like that. The façade of the court's building is a mere wonderful thing to look at.

There is, I believe, a great similarity between the outside appearance of the court and the United States' outside appearance as well. It is a false civilization. It is a beautiful building from outside but dark, lonesome, and harsh from the inside. The court transgresses against the humanity and rights of people without accepted justifications by the international norms and laws.

We sat in the court's restaurant while the attorney and her assistant took their lunch. I opened my backpack and held my wristwatch, which I really missed a lot. I realized the meaning and importance of time and its indications. I looked carefully at the watch and then placed it on my wrist. There are so many graces a person has, but one doesn't feel them unless he or she misses or loses them.

The weather was fine despite the cold freeze. The sun spread its rays on the place. The entire world turned grey in my eyes during the twenty days I was in jail. I felt only the presence of an armored car, cruel officers, rough uniform clothes, and boring scenes. I looked at the blue sky, the wide ocean, and its waves. I looked at the flying birds in the sky and the almost leafless trees. I looked at the faces of people around us.

The attorney and her assistant went to their office as soon as they finished their lunch. The office was a short walking distance from the court.

Temporary Residence

The attorney and I took a taxi to my new residence place on 215 West Newton Street, Copley House, Apartment 407. After ten minutes, we met the designated official by the court to be in charge of me and who was entrusted in fixing the electronic monitoring device in the apartment.

The attendant at Copley House led us to my efficiency apartment with a kitchenette, bed, sofa, television set, and small dining table with two chairs. There was also a private bathroom. The apartment was heated. There was a small storage room with a small closet, ironing table, iron, radio, and alarm clock. The room had a window that looked at a large garden and a very busy passageway. The trees of the garden were large, but their branches were almost leafless. The floor of the apartment was made of wood.

The rent of the apartment was five hundred dollars a week. I only had fifteen hundred dollars in cash, a thousand Saudi Riyals, a credit card, and an ATM card. I paid the rent for the first week. The apartment was appealing and pretty. I was happy to be there.

I needed at least three thousand dollars to cover the rent of the apartment, provided I stayed there for six following weeks until the end of the court hearings. It was 2:00 p.m. The defense attorney was happy to see the apartment in person because she only viewed its pictures on the Internet. The rent was high, as per the statement of the attorney. But the attorney was keen to get me out of jail.

Moreover, the living expenses in Boston are relatively higher than other areas.

The defense attorney asked the designated person from the court to take me to the grocery store to buy what I needed. She also asked him to show me the bank in the area to exchange money if I needed.

Friday was a new day and a historic turning point in my court case. I felt different. I was overwhelmed with happiness because I was able to call and receive incoming calls from whomever I liked. It was Friday at noon on January 23, 2004. I felt it was a glad tiding that I would be released from jail soon, though I was imprisoned in this apartment until the final sentence in my case was issued.

The attorney left the place. She informed me that she would see me on the coming Monday at 9:00 a.m., and she handed me a map describing the location of her office from there.

The release decree stipulated that I could meet the attorney for four hours on a weekly basis. I could also go shopping for food for three hours every Tuesday. It was a short period, but the person in need has to do what he has. The person from the court took me on foot to the Perdentall Mall. We searched for a bank or money exchange to exchange the sum I had.

I met a Moroccan girl who worked in the bank. Since my appearance looks like an Arab, the bank employee spoke to me in Arabic. The court representative interrupted the conversation, showed his official ID, and told her that he was the court's representative and he wanted her to address him and not me. I believe he was totally tasteless with his action.

The court representative took me to the bank that the Moroccan girl directed us to go to. Then he took me to Shaw's supermarket. We spent a little more than one hour there. The prices were extremely high. I bought a week supplies of food. I paid five hundred dollars for what I purchased. I remembered my country and its blessings. The same amount of money could buy a lot more than what I bought here. I carried what I purchased. The bags were heavy for my tired arms. The court representative walked carelessly in front of me.

This confirmed his cold feelings toward me beyond any doubt in my mind. We arrived the apartment after this short enjoyable trip to the market in Boston.

The place where the apartment is, it's one of the prettiest and high-class areas of modern Boston. Service areas from all directions surround it. As soon as I got comfortable in the apartment, the court official who was going to install the electronic monitoring device in the apartment began his work while I arranged the things I bought from the supermarket.

As soon as he completed the installation, he placed a monitoring device on my left wrist. This device could not be removed from my wrist except with a sharp tool. He warned me not to leave this place to any other site except for the designated locations I could visit; otherwise, they would take me back to jail again and sentence me to more severe penalties.

The electronic monitoring system is placed on either wrist of the hand or above the ankle of the foot, and it is connected to a telephone set. If the person who wears this monitoring device moves away to a certain distance out of the set range, the device would send an electronic signal to the programmed number, indicating that the monitored person moved from the designated place. The security officers then would initiate a search for such a person, arrest him, and take him to jail. That is what is meant by "under obligatory house arrest."

The court representative left the apartment. I stood at the balcony and looked at the public park. This park usually had several visitors during normal times. It started snowing. People began preparing themselves for the weekend. The sun set completely, and it was no longer seen in the horizon. A nice white coat of snow covered the ground and trees. Snow was on top of the cars, trees, pavements, roads, and even peoples' heads and shoulders.

I was attracted to a lady with her two children who were playing with snowballs in the park. I remembered my son Mohammed, who was two and half years old at the time, and my daughter Wasan, who was twenty-four days old. I also remembered their mother, my beloved wife. My eyes shed some tears. How would I not do so? They are the source of love and mercy.

My dear father-in-law told me that he did not tell my beloved wife about my situation because he was concerned about her health as a nursing mother to a young newborn baby girl. I totally agreed with him on that issue. Deep in my heart, I felt she felt that something was wrong and she knew about it. She usually feels my feelings. She knows if I am happy or sad. My intuition was right.

I went back inside the apartment and called my parents. They were very happy to hear my voice. They praised God the Almighty and thanked Him a lot. They felt that my call was a glad tiding signal of full release from jail. My dearest brother Yousef did not wait to get the news about my release and being placed under obligatory house arrest from me, but he rather contacted the attorney, and she told him about it. He always strengthened me. I remembered the kind and strong relationship of the two prophet brothers, Moses and Aaron PBUT, who supported one another.

True brothers at this time are a rare breed and grand treasure. In spite of his demanding job that requires intensive traveling, his part-time studies, his assignments, and his family activities and engagements, he did a lot for me.

The attorney's assistant told me, "Your brother Yousef loves you a lot. I wished I had a brother like him myself. He really cares for you."

God stated in Quran, TaHa 29-31, "Oh God. Please make a minister assistant for me from amongst my family; Aeron, my brother. Support me by him. Let him be my partner in all my affairs."

The attorney assistant was right when he congratulated me for having my brother Yousef. He suffered a lot for me. I won't forget our youth memories. They have their own best taste and flavor. May God the Almighty bless his heart soul, reward him, and grant him all the best.

I called my father-in-law and informed him that I was living in an apartment outside the jail. I informed him that I was waiting for the federal court hearings. It wasn't long before I heard the loving and longing voice of my dear beloved wife through the phone. She demonstrated strong hold of her emotions. I could see her tears pouring from her eyes from that long distance. I could feel that through her voice over the telephone line. Although she had lots of unuttered and unsaid queries, she displayed strong bravery. She was confused, suffering, and in pain to what had transpired.

She told me to have patience and perseverance, although she needed to be given patience and perseverance. She reminded me that, with patience, people have great rewards in the sight of God the Almighty. I praised God the Almighty for what she was and what she said. I was so grateful this Friday that I heard the voices of my parents. May God the Almighty protect them, the voices of my brother, wife, paternal aunts, and the rest of my nuclear family members.

After that call, I received a number of other calls. I was longing to recite the verses of the Glorious Quran. The Quran heals the pains, treats the wounds, and grants utmost pleasure. I feel that the Glorious Quran is a spring for my heart. God salvaged me and got me out of the prison. It is His virtue that I was released from a cell with an area of two square meters to a somewhat sizable apartment. I was deprived to see anything or anyone while in jail, and here I was. From the balcony of my apartment, I could see many people who passed by on a regular basis. I could see the trees, leaves, rain falling, and snow covering the ground.

In the prison, I was not allowed to call anyone or receive incoming calls. Here I was, and I had received over forty calls. I was not allowed a single visit, and here I was. I could receive people who would like to visit me for unlimited time. All praise is due to God the Almighty.

I called the Islamic Center in Boston. An American Muslim sister answered the call. I asked her about the prayer direction and prayer timetable, and she promised to send me the publication for

January and February. After I offered the *Isha*, late evening prayers, I tossed and turned over the bed. The mattress was a lot softer and comfortable than the solid steel bed and mattress that I slept on in the prison through the last three weeks.

This is another grace of God the Almighty that I can't thank Him enough for. I got up for *Fajr*, dawn prayer. It was the first time after twenty-one days that I could offer the dawn prayer on time, that is, the accurate time. I started thinking. *What would my destiny be? What would be my fate after this?*

Though I was happy to be out of PCCF and be in this apartment, I was still unsettled about the proceedings. I didn't know how to deal with the case. I was totally unfamiliar with the legal procedure, court trials, and litigation system in the United States.

My attorney requested the judge a monthlong postponement for the trial that she would declare her readiness. Otherwise, if she weren't ready, she would ask for another month postponement. The attorney told me later that, if it weren't for my family and work circumstances, she would have requested the postponement for two months to begin with. But she promised to try her best in my interest.

I spent Saturday and Sunday working very hard. I just stopped to offer my prayers or stop for few minutes to watch my little friend, the squirrel in the park very skillfully climbing the trees. All glory is due to God the Almighty who taught such a small animal such a wonderful skill. I answered the calls of my parents, family members, and friends who overwhelmed me with their kindness and generosity. Their emotional and physical stands had great impact on my life and me at this point. Their healing words helped heal my bleeding emotional wounds.

It is fantastic to feel that there are people surrounding you and wishing you all the best, extending their helping hands, prayers, supplications, and invocations that you can feel their impact on your life. I truly can't pay them back for what they had done except by saying, "May God the Almighty grant you all the best reward for what you had offered and done."

The First Meeting with Conrad at the Federal Defense Office

It was Monday morning of January 26, 2004, the pilgrimage season when people from all over the world would come to Makkah, Kingdom of Saudi Arabia, for pilgrimage. At 8:30 a.m., Boston time, I put a few slices of bread for my little squirrel friend on the balcony before I left the apartment. I left the apartment with a feeling of fear and hesitation. I walked quickly. It was the first time I walked alone in twenty-four days.

I went to the underground train station subway on Perdentall Street near the Commercial and Shaw's Center. I took train E from the green area heading to Park Street. The train stopped after four stops, and I transferred to the redline train heading to Braintree and Ashmont. After two stops, I got out of the train at South Station. I was at the beginning of Atlantic Road. The attorney's office was at 408 Atlantic Road. I walked over a nice, white carpet of snow. I was thankful to God the Almighty that I didn't get lost.

At 9:00 a.m., I was on the third floor by the Federal Defense Office. I sat in the reception, waiting for the arrival of the attorney. Upon arrival, she greeted me with her typical nice smile. She was fully vital and active. She took me in to her office looking at the Atlantic Ocean. I noticed through the window that the weather was full of heavy clouds. The rain was pouring constantly. Snow covered the streets. There were some natural scenes and beautiful pictures on the office walls. On her desk, there were photos for two children and a man. The children were her twin boys, and the man was her husband.

Although the office had central heating, the position of the office right at the ocean forced the attorney to keep her coat. As for me, I did not take off my coat to begin with. My attorney offered me a cup of hot coffee. I apologized to take it. I was mainly thinking about what she had to say about the details of my case and the appeal on Monday, February 23, 2004.

She sighed and then started to speak. "Let me explain some of the American federal law procedures. Twelve people would be picked from amongst a hundred applicants. Those are normal people. There would be doctors, engineers, general workers, and others among them. They would listen to the details of the hearings of case. The entire file of the case would be handed over to them. They would discuss it among themselves and have consultations in order to reach a unanimous decision. They are entitled to ask the judge any question about the case after calling the prosecutor and defense attorney."

The attorney's assistant came in and began listening to what she was saying.

"All the twelve jurors must unanimously agree on one decision, whether or not the defendant is guilty or not guilty."

"My goodness. I understood something, and I missed a lot of other things."

"Don't worry too much. I will explain more details to you later on."

The attorney reached a book on her desk. I had seen that book in the first meeting in the court building before I saw the magistrate judge on Monday, January 5, 2004. The attorney explained the penalty details and their possibilities. She repeated what she had told me before. Her assistant sat down and listened to what she had to say. The attorney noticed that I was surprised of what she read and said. She read that on my facial features.

I was surprised because the fate of my case was placed on the opinion and decision of twelve people and their conviction of what the prosecutor and/or defense attorney had to provide in terms of defense and evidences. These things may not reflect the real issues of the case itself. I did not get a convincing answer from the attorney. It was the nature of the federal American system. There are no other options or alternative. The most disturbing thing was what the attorney explained clearly.

"If the jurors didn't have unanimous agreement, they would be suspended. Another team of jurors would be elected, and the hearing would be repeated. I've been working for more than twelve years in court litigations. In my entire practical career, I did not record a reelection for another team of jurors."

The attorney's assistant wondered. "I know many clever attorneys who had a reelection of jurors in some of their cases."

The attorney confidently said, "Except me. You can make sure of that if you wish. It would be the opening session followed by several other sessions. I'll tell you the development in every session in order for the hearing to begin after four weeks, or else, the hearing would be postponed."

I expressed my concerns about the future of my job, my family, and so forth. I was neither depressed nor despaired. I just wanted to clarify the situation and express my true interest in expediting the hearing rather than postponing it.

"What are your expectations based on the information you have?"

"It is difficult to prejudge. I have a lot of work and research to do and preparations to make." The defense attorney looked at her watch. "We have approximately an hour before you should leave my office and return to the apartment, as per your schedule today." She began clarifying certain issues of my case.

I narrated the entire details of the story to her. I told her from the delivery of my wife until I landed in Logan International Airport. I related all the events that took place until the time I had met her before twenty-four days. She interrupted me, asking a few questions, and her assistant recorded all the notes. When it was time for me to leave, I was carrying my traveling backpack in my hand. The backpack had a hidden pocket that was not easily detected or seen.

I showed her that secret zipper, illustrating to her that, if I were the one who hid the firecracker materials, I could have put them in that hidden place. I could have used my intelligence, especially my backpack did not go through the x-ray examination machine at Logan International Airport.

I got up from my seat and greeted the attorney and her assistant to leave. I agreed with them that they would call me before the appointment to tell me when to meet again. I asked the attorney to explain the way back to the apartment for me. I left and went to the train station. I got off at Perdentall Station. I ran fast so I would not be late. I was afraid. I felt that many eyes were watching every move I made.

They had planted fear in my heart. My apartment was approximately three hundred meters away from the train station. I entered my apartment and locked the door behind me. I felt a little relaxed. I performed ablution and offered my prayers. I started reading in the Glorious Quran. The only time I stopped reading in the Glorious Quran was when I offered my prayers or looked for a little while through the window.

Many people passed through the park. I received several calls from my parents, wife, brothers, paternal uncles and aunts, maternal uncles and aunts, and a number of friends. The calls were comforting to me. All praise is due to God the Almighty at the beginning and end. Monday was over.

The days passed very slowly. The hours also passed extremely slowly. My schedule began by offering *Fajr*, dawn prayers, at approximately 4:00 a.m. I stayed awake until the sunrises. I went back to sleep until 9:00 a.m. I read in the Glorious Quran until noon or at times until early afternoon. At sunset time, I took my dinner. Then I read again in the Glorious Quran until the late evening prayer. I usually read in the case papers, which I had gotten from the attorney, for an hour or so. These documents had some reports and interrogations that the customs and federal agents completed. I reviewed these documents to discover if there were any false things written in them.

Of course, there was some time for meditating and thinking. I thought of what happened time and time again. There were some things nice and interesting, and there were painful things as well. However, I was very worried, confused, and frightened of what was going to happen. I often remembered God the Almighty and trusted Him with all my affairs.

Shopping and an Unexpected Visit

The preconditions of release from PCCF stated that the person would be under electronic surveillance, provided that the person would be permitted to go out for shopping, doing laundry, and so forth every Tuesday from 11:00 a.m. until 2:00 p.m. Of course to do all of that takes time, but these are the rules. Otherwise, the whip of the torturer is ready.

When it was time to go out for shopping came, I put on my coat, gloves, and hat and left Copley House. I came down from the third floor. I made sure several times that the apartment door was locked. I was extremely cautious and careful. I felt that even my steps were counted and monitored and my movements are recorded. Even if I did not talk, I felt that my voice was heard. A person who read the provided reports on the court would feel that he faced a professional criminal and one of the most skilled ones in criminology.

I crossed the street to go to the Perdentall Commercial Center. I was attracted to a bookstore on the second floor. I went into the bookstore to see the latest books and reading culture of the American people. I spent almost an hour in the bookstore. There were various shelves for magazines and various book types, including books on economics, politics, social studies, and specialized books in medicine, engineering, and else.

I moved on to the children's section. I sat and watched many mothers who accompanied their children to the bookstore. The mother picked what was suitable for her child. There were discussions between the mothers and their children. I listened to some of those innocent discussions. I wanted to explore and learn about the children upbringing method in this American open society.

The new books corner was right at the entrance of the bookstore. This section had some of the most controversial books. As I said, I spent more than an hour in the bookstore. But I could not visit every section in it during this first visit. I decided to come back again once more and not to make this visit the last one. It was a very attractive and rich bookstore with a great number of books.

I left the bookstore and took a quick round in the large shopping center. The mall had several menswear shops, women's boutiques, children's wear, and so forth. I went to Shaw's, the huge supermarket. I compared prices of the items with that in my home country. The prices were extremely high in comparison to that at home. I wanted to review the prices of the various items in order to plan what to buy for my needs. I picked a variety of items: vegetables, dairy products, carbohydrates, fish, fruits, and other items.

My trip took approximately two hours. I had one more hour left on my allotted schedule. I went to the barber and got a haircut. Then I preferred to go back to the apartment although the atmosphere was optimistic around me. No alarming things might cause me to be worried or concerned. But fear possessed me. I did not feel comfortable until I went inside the apartment and locked my door.

I immediately took a warm shower when I was released from jail last Friday, after the in-charge court official left the apartment. I enjoy warm baths. I was deprived from taking a warm bath while in jail. I could not take a bath in an open place while others are watching. I wonder how so-called civilized people take off their clothes and bathe naked in front and in the presence of others.

The inmates and security officers in jail also wondered why I continued to refuse to take a bath in open like that. I sat on the seat and looked through the window to the park. I always wondered when I saw people walking their dogs at such an early time. They walked and played with their dogs for almost an hour. Some people would bring a ball to play with their dogs. Others would bring a Frisbee, while others would bring bones for their dogs to play with and bite on.

When the walk was over, the person left the park. I very much wished to sit to record the expressions and feelings of those people toward their animals and what they do. They were kind to their animals and other animals in general. This is a matter that almost all faiths call for and encourage. But why do people have a double standard of measurement and treatment? What is the value of the human being whose rights are openly abused?

I thought and kept repeating several times that the reason to make such a big issue about my case and to announce it publically was for me being a Muslim and coming from the country of Islam, the Kingdom of Saudi Arabia. Several security agencies took special interest in my case, for example, the Customs Department, the Immigration and Naturalization authorities, Homeland Security, Federal Bureau of Investigations, Federal Defense Bureau, State Court Administration, US Embassy, Secretary of State (Ministry of Foreign Affairs], all types of media, and so forth.

My honorable attorney commented, "Last year, a young man who was under twenty years old came into the country with firecrackers and hashish drugs and was not referred to federal court. The case ended by fining the young man five hundred dollars (US) only. He was a young American boy. He was not a Muslim from the Kingdom of Saudi Arabia."

While I was sitting next to the window watching the movement of the squirrel on the branches of the trees, I heard knocks on the apartment door. I was frightened. Who could it be? Who wanted to visit me at this time? I heard the voice of the court official. He came into the apartment and examined everything very carefully.

He asked, "How was your trip today?"

"It was just fine."

"When did you leave the apartment?"

"I left a few minutes after eleven a.m."

"Where did you go?"

"I went to the shopping mall, bought some items that I needed, and cut my hair. Can you believe that I paid thirty-six dollars to cut my hair? Prices are very high in Boston."

"Where are your receipts?"

"Here they are."

"Well, keep them. We might need them for court auditing."

"Okay. I understand."

"Did you have any difficulties while you were outside?"

"No, everything went smoothly."

"Do you have any questions or comments?"

"No. Should I offer you a cup of coffee?"

"No, I have to leave."

The court official left the apartment. And again, as per the preconditions of the release from jail under surveillance, the coordinator had the right to pay a surprise visit to my apartment at any time. He also had the right to call me at any time he wished to do so, even after midnight. He was also entitled to ask me any question he liked. He was also entitled to inspect the apartment fully and ask any question he liked to ask. Otherwise, if I didn't do what he asked, I would be contradicting the set preconditions of the court.

Of course, I had the pleasure of calling my parents, wife, friends, and loved ones as well. I received a call from one of my friends who had a special touch on me. He advised me to stay up during the night before dawn and use the effective tool of supplication. He advised me to be truthful to God the Almighty when I stand on my feet and prostrate before Him. I felt a great impact of his advice on my life and situation. It made my life easier every step of the way. I had more patience and perseverance. And I was more determined and firm.

Looking for a Less Expensive Apartment and Meeting the Attorney

I made a phone call this Wednesday morning to the Islamic Center in Boston. I wanted to meet the director of the center. My inmate cell neighbor mentioned him to me, and he spoke highly of him and his good characteristics. The purpose of the call was to get his assistance finding an apartment that was less expensive of the one I was currently living in.

The Muslim sister who answered the phone informed me that the director was out of the country on a Hajj trip to Makkah and would come back two weeks after the end of Hajj season. I expressed my interest to her that I needed some assistance finding a more economical apartment between three hundred to three hundred and fifty dollars (US) a week. I made a few other phone calls for the same purpose.

One of the people I called apologized when he heard my story. Another one told me that he had shared rooms for rent. This was not at all acceptable as per the trial office. I had two other offers. One was too far and had no service facilities around it. The other offer was suitable, and it had its own telephone line. Of course, I needed a separate telephone line to connect the monitoring system device to it. I called the attorney's assistant, and I gave him the address and telephone number of the new apartment. This process took a lengthy time. One of the jail release conditions I signed on was not to exceed five minutes for the telephone call. Then I had to wait another five minutes and make another call, if I wanted to do so.

On Wednesday morning, a paper was placed under the door of my apartment from the housing administration. There was a mail delivery notice for me. It was a manila-sized envelope. My attorney had sent me that envelope. There were more documents related to my case hearing. It has reports from the FBI, Immigrations, and Homeland Security offices. I sat down and read the reports. I carefully examined them in order to discuss them with the attorney in her office in the next meeting. The first week passed.

I was afraid of the unknown future. I felt happy to receive comforting and encouraging calls from my family and friends at home. My country has people who felt the meaning of "There is no deity worthy of worship but God alone and Mohammed is His Prophet and Messenger." Those people wish good for others as they wish for their own selves. It is the grace of God that such people were offering supplications for me upon hearing my situation. We were in the first ten days of the twelfth Islamic month of the Islamic Hijri calendar. The good deeds on such blessed days are rewarded graciously, and they are more beloved to God the Almighty from the deeds performed on other days.

I often offered my humble, sound, and sincere supplications to God, especially when it rained and at the other times when supplications were hoped to be heard and fulfilled by God the Almighty. I knew for sure, deep in my heart, that the relief was coming soon. I felt:

- The impact of the prayers and supplications of my beloved parents in the sacred *Masjid* of Makkah
- The impact of sincere prayers and supplications of all my family members
- The impact of prayers and supplications of my dear beloved friends
- The meaning of the Hadith of God's Messenger PBUH, "The example of believers in terms of love, affection, mercy

offered from one to another is like that of one body. If one organ of the body ached, the rest of the body will sympathize with it in terms of becoming feverish and staying awake the entire night."[13]

What a beautiful feeling. When you feel that there are people who are happy for your happiness and feeling pain if you are suffering, you feel great.

My attorney called me and informed me about an appointment in her office at 9:00 a.m. on Wednesday, and she had gotten the permission from the court. I could leave the house forty-five minutes before the appointment. My attorney always reminded me to commit to the instructions and appointments.

I left the apartment a little after 11:00 a.m. I went to Shaw's and bought what I needed, and on the way back, I stopped at the dry cleaning and picked my clothes. I came to the apartment and paid the managing office the rent for the second and third weeks. I did not find a more suitable apartment until that date. I didn't know if the hearing would begin after two weeks from now or not. Now we were on Tuesday.

All my family members, on top of whom are my parents and all those who were closely following my case, were waiting to hear from me. I went to meet my attorney while all those people whom I mentioned were praying for me. I took the usual route that I took every time I went to visit the attorney. I entered the Federal Defense Office at 9:20 a.m. The attorney just walked into her office. It was still snowing as usual.

I spoke enthusiastically, "I did not notice this time that people were looking at me while I was coming."

"Your photo was not published in the media. Therefore, no one would know you."

---

[13]   This Hadith of God's Messenger PBUH is reported by Bukhari and Muslim.

"All praise is due to God the Almighty."

"Did you read the documents I sent to you by mail?"

"Of course I read them all."

"Is there anything missing from your backpack's contents?"

"Nothing except my passport and return ticket."

"They are in the possession of the court."

The attorney discussed her defense plan despite the fact that all indications were good. Yet she did not look assured or comfortable, as if she had thoughts about the surprises that the prosecutor would bring. She didn't answer my question if the court hearing would begin after two weeks or not. She did not answer many other questions of mine about her expectations of the results, as per the information available to her until that point.

She only made a remark. "We must work hard and diligently. I have too many things before I answer your questions."

By saying so, she stripped me from all enthusiastic and optimistic feelings I had at the beginning of meeting her on that day.

When the media asked the attorney about her opinion in the case, she frankly and openly said, "I expect that this case would demonstrate to you that the engineer came to attend a training course related to the nature of his work."

I went back to my apartment. My feet barely carried me. However, I could not control what was going on in my mind. I had a big confusion. I received several calls as soon as I got into the apartment. All the persons who called asked about the development in my case and asked God the Almighty to make it easy. One of the callers reminded me of the story of Prophet Joseph and how he remained several years in jail even though he was innocent. He suffered injustice, and he was accused in his own honor and integrity. He was away from his country, his parents, and family members. Yet he did not despair from God's mercy. I felt strong. Such calls strengthened me and brought peace and tranquility to my heart.

Days went by. I didn't know what was going to happen in the clever attorney's office. But I felt as if there were a workshop in her office. The two cavaliers in this workshop were the attorney herself and her young assistant.

On the third week of the case, the defense attorney was happy, and the situation was promising. She informed me that she could begin the hearing with full confidence after a week from that day. She found a university professor who expressed his readiness to give his testimony on the case. His résumé qualified him to be an expert on the case. He was a teaching professor in a university, and he worked as a consultant for explosives, firecrackers, and firework-producing factories.

It was the plan of God the Almighty that the professor had read the news of the young Saudi engineer who was arrested at Logan International Airport carrying firecracker samples in his possession. The professor communicated with the factory who was manufacturing items for a clarification on its danger. He later submitted his testimony in the court. This expert scientist explained the nature of those samples in detail. He was fully convinced that all what was being said about them was mere nonsense. He was equally convinced that the case did not need that much noise about it.

The attorney further asked for an appointment with the judge, and it was set for Thursday. This was happy news to me and a glad tiding that resulted, I believe, from the prayers of my two old, pious parents.

On Thursday, I headed to the courtroom along with the attorney and her young assistant. This was the first time I entered the court from its main official gate. The gate was decorated with elegant decorations bearing statements about justice, freedom, and equality. The court has a wonderful panoramic view over a lake that is connected to the Atlantic Ocean. The four fronts of the court have red color stones that add to the elegance of the beauty of the building.

We took the elevator to the fifth floor and headed to one of the halls there. At 10:00 a.m. exactly, the judge's secretary met us and informed us that she would arrive as soon as both the prosecutor and defense attorney would be there to hear the attorney's statement about her readiness to begin the hearing after one week from that day's date.

The attorney declared her provisional readiness in the presence of all witnesses whom she believed that their presence was in the interest of her defendant. She surprised me, along with all those who were present, that she requested the presence of witnesses from the Kingdom of Saudi Arabia, as per her memo. She also requested the facilitation of granting them an entry visa to the United States. Of course, the entry visa to the United States process requires more than eight weeks.

The judge apologized about the ability to intervene for granting the entry visa after the prosecutor intervened in this issue, claiming this issue took a long time due to lengthy procedures and security issues. They must do these things for the sake of homeland security and safety of the lands of the American nation. There was a surprise.

My attorney submitted a document issued by the court illustrating the issuance of a similar court order in a comparable case. This obliged the court and put the judge and prosecutor in an awkward position. They were lost for words. The judge accepted and approved the issuance, a court order to expedite the procedures. She requested the prosecutor to do his best to pave all difficulties in order to obtain the required visas. The attorney further asked the judge that the American government pay for all the expenses of the witnesses, that is, flight tickets and accommodations.

The judge commented that she never requested or did anything like that before. At that point, the clever attorney again handed the judge another document that illustrated that the government bore all the expenses incurred by the witnesses who came from outside the United States so long that their presence was in the interest of the case and it served justice.

Again, both the judge and prosecutor were unable to do anything, and they were helpless. The judge issued her sentence that the government bear all the expenses incurred by the witnesses for the case.

We left the court happily. I thanked the Almighty God for paving the work and removing the hurdles. We went together to the clever attorney's office. The active assistant of the attorney came along with us. A female law student was a friend of the attorney's assistant and a trainee in the Federal Defense Office. She came along with us. The law student attended the hearing of my case because she was interested in it.

The attorney held an immediate meeting with all parties concerned with the case. She discussed the arrangements for the hearing. The attorney planned a trip to Logan International Airport next Monday. She wanted to take photos for all the places I passed through before I was arrested on January 3, 2004.

I said good-bye to the attorney and left her office to go to the mall to buy a suit to wear on the day of the hearing in the court the next week. The attorney's assistant and the law student accompanied me. We headed to the mall on Washington Street in the downtown area. The significant role of the law student was very noticed in picking the right choice for the suit. When we finished, I said good-bye to both of them and headed toward my apartment.

As soon as I came in to the house apartment, I called my parents, wife, and brother. I told them what happened and informed them about all the progress and details. I consulted my parents whether to accept or reject a strange proposal of the prosecutor who told my attorney, "If your defendant comes to my office and apologizes for what he has done, I will drop one of the two charges against him."

Consequently, the attorney would be able to apply to the court to get a sentence for a six-month imprisonment for me with a suspension of the execution of the sentence. The prosecutor would support my attorney to obtain this sentence.

My attorney did not pay this proposal any attention at all. She expressed to him that she had to consult me about this before she gave him any type of reply, positive or negative.

"Dad, this is exactly what my attorney told me."

"Accepting injustice is awful, Essam."

"I'm tired of being away from home and family, Dad."

"Son, should a fault be treated by another fault?"

"No, Dad, but I am—"

"Son, why do you accept being defeated and weakened?"

"Dad, I am not weak, but I am tired of their cruel treatment."

"Son, your Lord, the Almighty, is watchful. He knows the most hidden information on everything."

"But, Dad."

"My dear son Essam, if you had done what they accused you with, then face your fate and result bravely. If you did so, then it is your own fault. But if you didn't do it, then don't accept any bargain at all. Don't bend your head. God the Almighty would surely make you victorious."

"Dad, you have brought me up on good principles. I am sure you know that."

"By God, I didn't have any doubts, even for a blink of an eye, that I force you to be patient, knowing that God's ease is very near."

My father wanted to teach me that:

A Man must be careful these days. He must be smart and intelligent. He should not grant his confidence, except for the one who is worthy of confidence, especially when he or she is outside his country and society. He should realize that the evil ones target him.

I called my wife, who in turn traveled with her family to Riyadh this Friday, to arrange for the travel and get the required visa from the US Embassy. I drafted a letter to my employer and Saudi passport authorities to request their assistance in renewing her passport.

When the attorney's assistant came to my apartment, he expressed his admiration with my courage and perseverance. He noticed a cheerful and optimistic smile on my face. I spoke to him about our traditions, and strong family ties and bonds. I spoke with him about my parents and family members as well. He expressed his admiration with the support extended to me by my family members.

He took my letter to send it quickly to my father-in-law. I had received every respect and moral support from my father-in-law. I learned later that he paid a big portion of the bond, while my family took care of the rest. I would never forget his stand with me for so long as I live. The attorney gave me her private mobile number, which she never used for business purposes. She informed me that I could call her at any time and in any emergency circumstances.

On Saturday, my brother Yousef, my wife, her father Musaed, his brother Saud, and my co-suffering colleague Mohammed waited in a long queue in front of the US Embassy in Riyadh, but they were told that the embassy had no instructions, none whatsoever, to issue them visas.

My father-in-law and my brother Yousef called me immediately right from the embassy. They wondered why the embassy had no instructions to issue them entry visas to the United States, though the attorney confirmed that the instructions and directions to do so were granted. The weather was desert cold in Riyadh. My wife was trying to hide her fatigue and weary feelings.

I called the attorney immediately on her day off. She was spending some time with her husband and her two twins. She tried in turn to make few calls about this issue. But she called me later and told me that there was no use now because it was the weekend holiday. She promised to intensify her calls to the people in charge on Monday morning.

Time was passing too quickly. I didn't know what to do. My attorney told me that she was going to request permission to increase my visits to her office as of next Monday. She wanted to make the visit last four hours. As for my wife, she was able to renew her passport within a few hours, only due to the immense attention of the officers in charge, on top of who was HRH Nayef bin AbdulAziz and HRH Mohammed bin Nayef.

On Monday, I went to visit the office of the clever and wonderful attorney. Again, before I left the apartment, I put some bread slices for my little friend, the squirrel on the balcony. I met the attorney and her assistant. She explained to me what would happen in the court and the method of choosing the jurors. She further explained the method of questioning of the prosecutor to the witnesses. She informed me that the young man I met on the plane while I was coming from Frankfurt to Boston on the flight decided to be a witness in my case.

We went together to Logan International Airport. This was the first time I entered the main front halls of the airport. We waited for the arrival of the prosecutor who, as soon as he arrived, gave his instructions to officials in charge at the airport not to answer any question my attorney asked.

We went on a round to visit all the places where I passed through when my flight arrived at the airport. We went to the gateway and immigration and secondary inspection areas. The attorney's assistant had a digital camera, and he took shots of all the places as per the instructions of the attorney. We went to the secondary inspection area and customs area. I pointed to the location of the room where I was interrogated and the back door I had been transferred through to the police station. This door was close to the luggage area.

A couple customs officers and Homeland Security officers accompanied us in our round. I could still remember the kind features of the old customs officer. The battery of the digital camera became fully out of charge while the attorney's assistant was taking pictures of the places. The old customs officer extended his help by providing batteries and handing them to the attorney's assistant.

The officers were not too happy with what he did. When the attorney's assistant completed his picture-taking process, the prosecutor took the storage card of the camera, placed it in an envelope, and sealed it properly.

The attorney aimed to draw a full plan for my movement throughout the various halls of the airport in order to explain that to the jury. She also wanted to see some specific places there. Before she left the airport, she asked to see the place where the customs explosive officer from the FBI tested one of the three found items.

My attorney was shocked. The place where the test was done was the airport runway close to the airplanes. She insisted on taking a photo shot for that place.

I commented to myself, "Didn't the expert fear that the sample would explode and affect the safety of the planes and those in the vicinity? If I weren't an Arab from the Kingdom of Saudi Arabia, wouldn't they have a different scenario and formula, along with a altered way of treatment and handling?"

We all left the scene after she took the required photos.

The attorney also made some phone calls and advised me to call my family quickly in order to go to the embassy. Monday, Tuesday, and Wednesday passed by, almost eventless. Thursday, Friday, Saturday, and Sunday were a long weekend for both the United States and KSA. These days also passed eventless. My family members, however, went on a regular basis to the US Embassy, hoping to get their entry visa to the United States.

On Saturday evening, the skilled attorney was able to contact a senior officer who expressed interest in offering assistance. She expressed to my attorney that she was the only one who had the executive authorities in this field. The attorney expressed her surprise that things were going in such harmonious and accurate planning.

The attorney called my family. I did call them as well. They rushed to the US Embassy and settled among themselves that my wife, her father, her uncle, and my friend Ossama would come to the United States. Others excused themselves due to personal reasons. As for my friend Mohammed, the embassy did not grant him an entry visa. I was told that he was very sad and he tried his best to convince the counselor at the visa section with the due importance of his travel. There was no hope. The instructions didn't allow him to get an entry visa to the United States. My father asked me to list his name on the witnesses' list. Mere words could not capture or express parents' emotions.

My father is a good-hearted man with great merits and sweet talk and words. He has a vast wealth of experience. The incident increased his faith in God the Almighty and deepened it. He often repeated a famous Islamic phrase, "God suffices me. He is the best trustee." He often told me, "Son, be patient and often offer prayers. Often offer remembrance of God the Almighty. Don't be despaired from God's mercy." He often said, "Son, God the Almighty will soon release you from prison. Don't worry. God would remove your worries. God would return you home, sound and safe Don't you worry." That is his faith that he demonstrated. That is my great father.

My mother has a kind and merciful heart. She is highly emotional and easily moved to tears. In spite of her illness, she took the hardship to go to the Grand Holy Mosque of Makkah upon hearing the news about my arrest in order to offer supplications and prayers to God the Almighty for me. She went there during the pilgrimage season. She held the cover of the holy shrine of Kabah, asking God the Almighty to ease my situation and relieve my worries and pains. She advised me every time she called or we spoke over the phone to be patient.

She often said to me, "I ask God the Almighty to enable me to see you soon."

Both my parents often tried very hard to ease the situation for me. They used kind and soft words. They shed tears while talking to me. I often heard my mother's brokenhearted voice while talking to me on the phone. Oh God, please reward them highly for their sufferings for me. Oh God, bless their hearts and grant them the best of both worlds. Oh God, please be kind to them as they were kind to me when raising me as a little child. Oh God, please enable me to be kind to them throughout my entire life. Oh God, enable me to be loyal to them for the rest of my life. Yes, indeed. God the Almighty saved me and salvaged me due to their blessed supplications while they offered supplications in their prostration to God the Almighty. They offered supplications every time they could. All praise is due to God the Almighty. He is the graceful and deserving of all praise.

Oh God, please enable me to provide them the best care at their old age in this life as they provided the best care for me while I was little. Oh God, please preserve them and make them amongst your pious and righteous slave-servants of yours.

The First Day:
The Beginning of the Court

It was Monday morning, February 23, 2004. It was a great day in the course of the court hearing raised by the government of the United States against myself. Before going to the court, I stood before God the Almighty, the owner of all affairs, the one who fulfills all the needs and responds to the brokenhearted people when they call sincerely upon Him alone. I directed my heart sincerely to Him. He is the best one to hear and respond.

I left my apartment at 7:30 a.m. It was the first time I left my apartment at this early hour. I left some pieces to eat for my little friend, the squirrel. It liked slices of bread. I believe that there is a reward for feeding every living, nonharmful soul. I went to the Federal Defense Office. I met the attorney at 8:15 a.m., Boston time. It was 4:15 p.m., Riyadh time.

The attorney made a few phone calls and lent me her husband's necktie to wear. On our way to the court, she informed me that the jury selection process would be done at 9:00 a.m. She further told me that she and her assistant examined one of the three samples and were truly surprised, the sample was too little to be significant and it did not need such a fuss and noise about it.

The attorney continued her talk to me after the jury's selection process. The court session would begin shortly after. My wife, her father, her uncle, and my friend Ossama would arrive at Boston at 4:00 p.m. tomorrow, Tuesday. We entered the court after passing a security gate and went up to either the fifth or sixth floor, as far as I remember.

We found the prosecutor for the first time, along with his assistant. We also found a translator who the court assigned based on the request of my attorney. She wanted him to be there to translate the difficult legal terms that I might not understand or be familiar with. He introduced himself to me. He was a Lebanese American who lived for over twenty years in the United States. His spoken Arabic was broken as if he reflected the communication patterns between the Arab and Western societies.

There was no time to change or exchange him with another person. He sympathized with my case as he listened to a portion of it as I told him. He advised me to speak slowly and confidently and to take my time when I answered the questions of the court. After a few moments, the judge arrived along with her secretary, clerk, and court commission. She gave her instruction to both parties, the prosecutor and defense. The court's representative who was responsible for the electronic monitoring handed in his report about the last four weeks as I was under electronic monitoring and mandatory stay.

The pretrial officer in charge proved no legal violations on my part. At that time, the judge ordered one hundred persons, male and female, for the process of selection of jury. All those in the courtroom stood up in a greeting motion to them. The nominated jury sat in their assigned seats. We all exchanged looks at each other.

The judge addressed the nominated jury and gave her instructions to them. We all listened to her for more than thirty minutes. At the end of her speech, the judge herself made them repeat the oath after her. As for the interpreter translator, who was sitting with us in the defense corner next to the attorney and me, he went into a deep sleep. He snored to the extent that the judge ordered him from her bench to wake up.

He turned to me with a smile on his face. "Was I really sleeping?"

The judge dictated a huge amount of guidance and instructions to the nominated jury that helped them deliberate the right decision after listening to the entire details and circumstances of the case. They would listen to the witnesses and statements of the prosecutor and defense attorney, all the concerned parties. My attorney handed me a list of all the nominated jury for the case. The list had the names, addresses, and positions of the suggested jury. Thirteen jurors— twelve essential members and one reserve—would be selected.

The jury would be present to listen to all the litigation from all concerned parties and all the details of the case. The assigned jury had to give a full consensus about whether the defendant was guilty or not.

The defense attorney and prosecutor stood at the right side of the judge's bench. The judge managed and directed both concerned parties about the selection process of the jury. More than thirty nominees were excluded from the selection process, including those who had special circumstances or negative feelings about the case or defendant himself.

The prosecutor was given the first priority to select jurors. He had the right to select the first juror for the case, as per the rules of the federal court laws. The prosecutor and his assistant selected the first juror for the case. Both parties must agree on the selection of the jurors. The selection of the jury was a mere personal feeling of the selector, either pro or con. The attorney felt that the jury selection process was merely absolute luck.

As for me, I felt that God would help in this selection as He deemed fit and favorable. I was confident that God would enable these jurors to announce my complete innocence and enable me to go back home to my family, safe and sound of all blemishes.

One interesting thing that transpired during the jury's selection process, which lasted a few hours, there was a light-colored woman among the jury who was smiling every time I looked toward her. She had weary looks. When the number of the jury to be selected was completed, that weary-looking woman was not selected. The attorney's assistant noticed that the woman was upset because she was not selected. She made several nods to that effect.

The intelligent attorney's assistant turned to me later. "Hey, man, what did you do to that young American lady?"

In fact, I was indulged with much deeper things than looking at that woman and her moves. The selection process in reality took a long time to complete.

When the selection process was completed and the quorum was achieved according to the American Constitution, six men and six women were selected. As for the thirteenth juror, she was a reserve one. A blonde, middle-aged Catholic woman was among the jury. The list of the jury had two black women, one married to a Muslim whose name was AbdulAziz. As for the other woman, she possessed a high degree in law and defense. Her husband worked previously as a judge in one of the American court system. There were teachers, university students, engineers, and regular citizens amongst the selected jury.

It was truly a wide spectrum, as my attorney expressed. I felt that such selection was divinely done and arranged. It was the result of the prayers and supplications of my two old parents and my pious wife, along with the prayers of the righteous who knew me and prayed for me.

We moved to another smaller courtroom. Everyone took his or her assigned seat. The judge repeated her instructions to the prosecutor and defense attorney to commit to the rules and regulations that were explained before.

She addressed the jury. "Ladies and gentlemen, you will hear many objections and arguments. You will notice several interruptions. You will see many sidebar meetings among the judge, prosecutor, and defense attorney. You have all the rights to explore all exhibits and evidences of the case. I advise you to jot down your notes and comments that would help you later on to give the proper sentence over the case."

At that time, the judge permitted the litigations and trial opening. The prosecutor stood up and explained the situation to the jury. He took approximately ten minutes in his opening presentation.

The defense's turn came. The attorney was wonderful in every word and expression she used. Even her body language was wonderful as well. I noticed the reactions on the faces of the jury.

She said, "Ladies and gentlemen, you will listen to a case that, at the end, you will not know the doer or the person who committed the crime. But at the end, you will discover that my defendant is not the doer. I confirm to you that you will listen and hear the truth and nothing but the truth."

The attorney sat down, and I noticed that the jury wished that the attorney did not stop talking.

The prosecutor's team sought the permission of the judge to read a clarification agreed upon by both parties: the prosecutor and defense that talked about my personal CV, my position, the reason for traveling to the United States, the type of visa that had been authenticated to be a legal one and the hotel reservations, the manufacturing company that would offer the training, and so forth. This was a suggestion proposed by my attorney to the court in order to shorten the trial and litigation times.

The first day of the trial ended. The interpreter sought permission to leave and come back on Wednesday or Thursday in order to do the interpretation for my wife. It was exciting to see that a good number of federal public defense attorneys attended the opening session of the trial and followed with great interest what both, the prosecutor and defense attorney, had to say. They did not hide their admiration with the way of presentation of the skilled defense attorney presenting her case. Several members of Boston's media attended and covered the court trial on that day.

Upon returning to the office, the attorney received praise and compliments from her colleagues and boss. They were happy to see the progress of the case. We discussed the events of the entire day at court. The attorney's assistant presented his observation about the proceedings. I returned to my apartment at 7:00 p.m. I ate my dinner and received a call from my parents, who were praying for me. After I finished my chores, I went into a deep sleep. It was a very eventful and tiring day. It was a new and unique experience for me, though it was very tough and unfair.

I got up early on the morning on Tuesday. I needed to address God the Almighty. At the set time to visit the attorney's office, I left the apartment. We headed from there to John Joseph Moakley's Courthouse. I was pushing the cart with all the documents of my case litigations while entering the court.

The attorney, her assistant, and the trainee attorney in the Federal Defense Office, who was also a law student in the university, addressed my attorney. "I had a dream yesterday where I saw Engineer Essam happily telling me that the case was over and he won the case...."

The attorney immediately turned to her and asked her to stop talking and not complete her dream. We went through the customary check at the gate, and we entered the court.

The Second Day: The Witnesses

We entered the courtroom to resume the case litigations. Upon the arrival of the judge, along with her secretary, the court scriber, and court commission, and prior to the entry of the jury, the attorney requested the judge for a private sidebar meeting, a normal practice in the American federal court system. Both sides of the defense and prosecutor took their stands in the specified locations. The jury was requested to come into the courtroom. The judge and both the defense and prosecutor parties sat down after all the jury was seated.

The prosecutor requested his first witness to come to the witness stand. After taking the oath, the witness began giving his testimony. While my attorney discussed the case with him, it was clear that he didn't base his testimony on an eyewitness but rather on the statements and eyewitness of others. It was sufficient that I didn't see that person at all and he didn't see me except at the courtroom for the first time on January 5.

The second witness was the customs inspector of French descent, an American citizen. He was about thirty years old. He took the three tiny items found in my backpack. He looked pathetic while offering his testimony. He stuttered a lot while answering the questions of the prosecutor. He was unsure of his answers. The prosecutor asked if he could identify me in the court or not. His reaction was unexpected. He avoided looking in my direction.

The skilled defense attorney asked about the report that he wrote about the case. She also asked him further about the conflicting information in the report that he wrote. It was clear that his boss wrote the report, not him. He only provided him with some information about what happened.

My attorney directed a knockout strike. "Shouldn't you have reviewed the report that was written under your name?"

The witness didn't have any comment or reply. Some people usually stutter when they approach the truth, while others stammer when they approach the false and lying circle. All glory is due to God the Almighty, who had shaken this witness and clarified the truth. My attorney was satisfied with directing these questions, and she did not pose any other questions. The jury was surprised with what they heard. As for me, I was totally shocked. All matters were going positively in my favor. All praise is due to God the Almighty.

It was time to listen to the third prosecution witness, a man over fifty-six years old. This customs supervisor confused the judge with his contradicted statements. Thus, she requested him to leave the witness stand, stand before the jury, and explain what happened in detail at Logan International Airport. In fact, this made him much more confused.

The witness was perspiring a lot, though the weather was cold. He was barely able to talk. All the jurors thought that this witness was drunk or so. He couldn't explain how he met me and what transpired between both of us at the airport. This witness left the witness stand, followed by unsatisfactory looks of the jury and all who listened to his testimony. The attorney didn't direct a single question to this witness.

The attorney went to her office during the lunch break. Her assistant went to arrange the reception of my wife, her father, his brother, and my colleague, Ossama Abbass. I took a seat at one side of the court, and I offered supplications to the Almighty God.

At 1:30 p.m., when all the people convened again, the case litigations were resumed. The prosecutor requested his witness to come to the witness stand. The witness was the immigration and law enforcement officer. He was in his early forties. He had Western features and of middle height.

He was along with his boss when they interrogated me at Logan International Airport on January 3, 2004, and he took the oath at the witness stand. He testified that I told his boss and him that my wife packed my backpack. He also heard me deny any knowledge about the tiny items that the customs inspector, the first witness, took out of my backpack. He further confirmed that I told them that the tiny items looked like crayons and I did not say that they were crayons, per se. This backed up the reality of my claims

The prosecutor called upon his fifth witness, the lab technologist. His testimony summarized his method of analysis of the materials and the results he got. The expert professor listened to the testimony. He whispered in the ear of the defense attorney, who requested the court to review the notes written by the analyst. The analyst's testimony was a pure, detailed, scientific statement. I could not understand or follow up on the subject because of the nature of its terminology. But the professor and attorney both were following up closely. The end of this testimony terminated this court session of Tuesday. This session was full of glad tidings.

There was a dangerous turn in the case. The prosecutor had only one more witness, the explosive expert, to call. The prosecutor planned his testimonies to present three explosive experts, but my expert and shrewd defense attorney objected before the beginning of the litigations. She requested the judge to only have one explosive expert in order to avoid any ambiguity by the jury staff. Listening to three testimonies plays with the jury's emotions and may have a negative impact on them. This would also waste the time of the court. It was God's favor that the judge approved the attorney's objection.

I walked quickly to reach the Federal Defense Office. I was even racing the ground itself. My attorney expressed her feeling of happiness for the progress of the case at the court.

I repeated to myself, "All glory is to God who turns the hearts of people as He likes."

I had an overwhelming happiness. I was about to meet the twin of my soul, my soul mate, my beloved wife. She sacrificed her peace and security by coming to the United States for my own sake.

As soon as I reached the third floor where the defense attorney's office was located, I headed to office 303 to say hello to my beloved wife, the mother of my elder boy Mohammed and younger girl Wassan.

My wife's voice was a mixture of cries and weeping. I couldn't understand what she had said. Our hearts were trembling hard. There was almost a complete silence. The tears expressed the deep emotions and love. We hugged each other for a long period of time. The people around us were in tears because of this touching scene. There were no words heard, and the speech was for the tears only. I was finally able to see my honest, sincere, patient, and loyal wife. I also hugged my father-in-law; Uncle Musaed, the one with the great heart; and his brother, Uncle Abu Raihan, who is known for his noble stands.

I further hugged my dear friend and colleague, my close friend and companion for the past nine years, Ossama Abbass. Everyone was moved with this meeting. The attorney was in tears to see us in such a warm meeting-and-greeting situation. The same was said about her aide and law student. My wife, father-in-law, his brother, and my friend all got together to support the case in the court. They felt the sincerity, loyalty, close ties, and strong emotions of all of us. We were a close net, like one body's organs. If one organ suffers, the rest of the body would support it by being feverish.

I should mention here my dear beloved wife, my best garment for my body and soul. I would like to talk about her role in offering the best types of support. She presents the best material mental and spiritual support. She proves she would sacrifice herself for my sake. She doesn't mind the results, whatever they are. She supports me mentally, spiritually, and otherwise.

She is one the best wives. She is one of the best loyal and kind persons, and she is one of the best companions in this life. I ask God the Almighty, as He enabled me to meet her, have her company, and enjoy it in this life to enable me to have her company in the hereafter as well.

We sat to talk, but I didn't know where to begin. I talked about my parents, the weather, the court and the litigations, and so forth. The attorney interrupted us and requested Engineer Ossama and AbuRaihan to be prepared for a meeting with her today in preparation for the court session on Wednesday. Time passed so quickly. We must be prepared.

The skilled attorney put a great effort on the case. The words of gratitude that we presented to her were insufficient for the great efforts. Until now, I still pray from the core of my heart for this blessed attorney, hoping she would be guided to the niche of God's light. The attorney's aide accompanied my father-in-law, his brother, and my dear friend Ossama to the hotel, which was only five minutes away from the Federal Defense Office building.

I accompanied my beloved wife to the apartment, approximately thirty minutes away from the same place. When we reached the apartment and closed the door, we sat for a long time talking. My wife told me about her feelings prior to the incident. She reminded me how uncomfortable she was about the trip. She further reminded me with the good-bye scene, which was unusual for me. She mentioned that she told her mother about her mysterious inner feelings about this trip. She told me about the dreams she had while I was gone. I listened with interest to all what she related to me.

I have known my beloved wife and her transparent feelings. I have known her truthfulness. I did not doubt anything she said. She related the feelings of my parents and family members and their longing for me. She mentioned the stands of some of our neighbors and mutual friends as well. I felt how tired she was after this lengthy trip. She spent a week of hardships before the travel. She stood long hours at the gate of the US Embassy in Riyadh. She talked about our two children, Mohammed, who was two years and ten months, and our daughter Wasan, who just completed her second month at that time.

I had left my daughter when she was only five days old. She told me about many other things. She encouraged me to be patient and have perseverance. She went on and on, comforting me and encouraging me.

The Third Day: Litigations Continue

I put on my clothes on Wednesday morning. I wore the clothes that my wife brought with her for me. We went together to the Federal Defense Office. We held hands together. My wife and I couldn't believe that we had met again and we were walking together. She was afraid despite all what she tried to encourage me to have patience and perseverance. She pretended to have a strong will and super control over her emotions. My father-in-law Musaed, his brother Saud, and my dear friend Ossama were waiting for us, along with the attorney and her aide.

We exchanged greetings and headed to the courthouse. After everyone took his place in the courtroom, the judge entered the room. Both teams, the defense attorney and prosecutor, along with the judge, discussed the case for a few minutes. Each party took its assigned place. The judge permitted the jury members to come into the courtroom.

The prosecutor requested the judge to present his final witness, a largely built person with a big-sized head with a very suspicious look on his face. He worked for sixteen years as a police officer in Massachusetts, and he worked as an explosive destruction officer at Logan International Airport since eight months approximately.

The witness said, "On Saturday, January 3, 2004, I received a request from the immigration department in the international terminal at Logan International Airport to give my opinion based on my previous technical experience in the explosives field on three, cylindrical, yellowish, tiny items. On the capsules, there was some writing of combination of letters and numbers. The writing was in black. The code written on the capsules was K0201. These items were taken out of the passenger Essam AlMohandis while being inspected. Upon examining the items, I concluded that the material was a mixture of phosphor and other chemical minerals, a pyrotechnic mixture. In order to ensure my findings, I took the inner content of one of the items to the runway and lit it. It was in flames immediately upon touching the lit match. The fire extinguished quickly afterward."

He described the explosive materials as stated in Webster's dictionary. "Any material that is placed in a potentially breakable container, whether hard or solid or liquid material with burning potentiality. The wick could snap when it reaches the liquid or solid flammable material. It may be carried personally or thrown."

He repeated his statements in several different ways, adding and deleting or altering several technical terms.

When he concluded his testimony, my skilled defense attorney posed some questions to the witness. "Do the samples that you examined look like regular fireworks? Does it resemble crayon? Where was it manufactured? Did you contact the manufacturing company to inquire about the nature of that material and its flammability's impact? Do you know how long it would burn?"

One wouldn't believe the scene of this huge person after he received these questions. How he did change and blushed. The defense attorney asked him about the weight of the materials in grams and its quantity. He could not give an exact answer or figure. He wanted to mislead the jury and make them believe that the quantity was big. He could not play around with a smart and intelligent attorney.

The attorney asked, "Is the material the size of a small teaspoon?"

He stutteringly said, "It was less than that."

She asked him about the duration of burning. He replied that it did not exceed a few seconds, but he did not give any definite number. She requested him to reread the definition of the explosive material according to Webster's dictionary.

Then she commented on his statement. "Wax candle is considered flammable. It could lead to fire. Can we include it under this definition? The same applies to a cigarette."

But his answers were confused and shaky without any sound scientific basis. He just submitted his personal opinion and practical experience about the matter.

The final question that the attorney asked the witness was, "Is it permitted to carry a matchbox or cigarette lighter to the airplane?"

His answer was negative, as per the rules. The attorney referred to some statistics issued by Logan International Airport that contradicted his testimony. The attorney did not ask any further questions. She just wanted to illustrate a few things to the jury. All glory is due to God who inspired her to pose such intelligent questions.

After the sixth witness of the prosecutor, the defense attorney requested her witnesses to come to the witness stand. Her first witness was the young American citizen who related the story of the trip from Frankfurt to Boston. He talked about my behavior during the trip and the discussions we had on the plane. He talked about the nature of both of our jobs. He even told them an interesting thing when I offered him my piece of chicken when the meal was distributed to the passengers. This indicated his kindness and good personality. His testimony confirmed that he did not notice any suspicious activities done by me. He also referred that I left my seat on the plane twice, once to go to the bathroom and another time to get the hotel reservation paper to guide me how to get to the location of the hotel and what the best transportation means would be to take.

The attorney called my dear friend, Ossama Abbass, to the witness stand. He offered a light, delightful, and very spontaneous testimony. Ossama knew me for approximately nine years. We were very close and intimate friends. He mentioned many good things about my personality based on the close and direct association with each other. He related to the jury that he was my immediate supervisor for the last four years.

The third witness, the expert professor, reminded me of my university professors. He was tall and bald in the center of the head. He was light-haired at both sides of the head. He was skinny, calm, and very convincing with a strong argument. He wore eyeglasses that indicated a professional scholastic look.

The professor presented an introduction about firecrackers and fireworks. He further talked about his scientific expertise as a designer, manufacturer, and consultant of fireworks for many large fireworks factories around the world.

He addressed the attorney. "I had read by chance about the incident in the newspaper. I sent an email to the manufacturing company out of scientific curiosity about the nature of the explosive materials of the said case. I didn't imagine that I would be a witness in the case."

The professor explained in detail what he wanted to illustrate, indicating a documented and authoritative scientific viewpoint. He rebutted the testimony of the prosecutor's witness who was the last witness. The professor's testimony lasted over forty-five minutes. The prosecutor displayed further documents and analysis, but my attorney objected because she didn't see or read them before. She wanted to ask the opinion of the expert professor before she said anything about them. She asked for extension until the next day, Thursday.

During lunch, the defense attorney went along with the professor to an office in the courthouse to read the documents and ask the professor about his opinion. We went to offer our prescribed daily prayers.

My dear friend Ossama insisted on inviting us for lunch in the Park restaurant. It was located half the distance between John Joseph Moakley Courthouse and the Federal Defense Building. It was known for its seafood. It was a nice restaurant, and we enjoyed our lunch. The restaurant's owner talked to us about the popular Boston lobster.

We returned to the court after an hour to resume the proceedings of the case. We met the attorney and the professor. They both had wide smiles on their faces.

The attorney said, "There is nothing of substance in what we had read even worthy of mentioning or rebutting. I would settle for what has been said in the court."

When all the concerned parties settled down in their seats in the court, the case expert sat on the witness stand for less than ten minutes to answer the questions of the prosecutor. The judge permitted the court's technical team, along with the person in charge of the remote teleconfeance setup, to make a long-distance call to the Kingdom of Saudi Arabia. All the equipment was brought into the courtroom, and they initiated a call to Riyadh, Saudi Arabia. There was a technical problem with the connectivity. It was 3:00 p.m. in Boston and 11:00 p.m. in Riyadh.

The technical team looked impatient. I started getting worried myself. They attempted to call at least fifteen times. This was very annoying and disturbing. It was a difficult time for me. The US Embassy at Riyadh denied my colleague and trip partner, Mohammed AlHayyan, the entry visa to the United States. The prosecutor tried several times to object to the testimony via the telecommunication equipment. But the defense attorney tried very hard to convince the court and judge. The refusal to grant a visa was issued by the US government through the embassy in Riyadh, and it was not by the witness. Mohammed was very keen and interested to attend as a witness. His name was on the list of witnesses to offer their testimonies to the court and jury.

I thought of the technicians' attempts to call. We had made several phone calls with our colleagues in Riyadh, who exerted every effort to make the court call a success. The people in charge recommended putting every effort to make the call a successful one. My colleagues ensured that all the telecom equipment at Riyadh was in excellent shape to receive the call and pass it through. The technical telecom team at the Kingdom of Saudi Arabia shared some instructions and advices to the technical team at Boston's court.

On the twenty-fifth attempt to call, I heard the voices of the Saudi telecom team through the equipment. In a few moments, I was able to see my colleague Mohammed AlHayyan's face via the satellite communication equipment, along with other faces. I noticed that my brother Yousef was also present with the people there. The two teams exchanged the greetings over the video conference.

The judge and jury members were all ready after waiting for forty-five minutes to establish contact with the witness in the Kingdom of Saudi Arabia. Several attempts were made. Finally, God's help was granted, and the call came through.

The judge commented, "Technology eases the situation and brings the distances closer. But it may cause some embarrassing situations."

My attorney requested the permission to pose her questions to the witness, Mohammed AlHayyan. Everyone noticed how happy the judge was to see herself on the satellite telecommunication equipment. The judge ordered all those present in the room set up for testimony at Riyadh to leave the room except for the witness alone.

She addressed him directly. "We are talking with regards to case number PBS 04-40001 where the American government sues Mr. Essam AlMohandis. The defense attorney requested your testimony on the case."

The translator requested the witness to repeat the oath after him, which he did. The defense attorney began asking her questions. The questions revolved around our trip, how we met, and who drove us to the airport. She asked about my behavior, the inspection points that we passed through, and so on. The testimony was somewhat interesting. At times, the witness spoke in English, and at other times, he switched to Arabic. The judge was somewhat confused. But she wanted to make him feel comfortable.

What made my colleague switch back and forth between the two languages was really the poor translation job presented by the translator. He did not make much sense translating in both languages.

At the end of Wednesday, a very eventful day, my wife and I—along with her father, his brother, my colleague Ossama, and the attorney who was very successful in doing her job—left the court. After we were a far distance from the court, I asked the attorney about her impressions about the case. Her reply was ambiguous. She only alluded that the case was going well. I noticed with the attorney that she liked to focus on what she was doing and didn't like to jump to conclusions quickly.

I blamed myself for asking. I believe that God the Almighty is the best caretaker of all things, and I should trust Him with all my affairs with all my heart and all my might. We rested for a while at the attorney's office, and the attorney requested to sit with my father-in-law's brother. When she completed the interview with him, she asked for my wife.

At about 6.30 p.m., my father-in-law called from the hotel. He informed the attorney's assistant that he and my colleague Ossama were on their way to the attorney's office. The attorney's assistant asked me to go through the back door and open the door for them to let them in the building. The main gate of the building is locked after the official working hours.

They were late in arriving. I tried to keep the door open while waiting for them to come. A police squad car passed by, and one of the officers came down. He asked what I was doing at that time in this building and why the building door was open. I was shocked with his yelling. I was afraid that he would take me along in the police car and place me in custody without the knowledge of my attorney. I was afraid that they would direct further accusations to me.

I told him what I was doing. He asked about my attorney, and I told him who she was and where her office was on the third floor of the same building. He commanded me to walk in front of him until we reached the attorney's office. The attorney's assistant explained to the officer what happened and said that he asked me to go down to open the door for the concerned people.

The police officer left the area when he was convinced. I was sweating with worries, though it was a cold season. When my father-in-law and my colleague arrived, the attorney's assistant went down and opened the door for them to avoid any unexpected situations. And after we were all done with the active attorney, my father-in-law, his brother, and my colleague Ossama headed to the hotel while my wife and I went to our apartment. I told her what happened and the course of the case. She was worried about sitting on the witness stand. She is bashful and highly shy.

She was worried about facing a large crowd of people. She did not know where to keep her face and at whom she should look. It was truly a difficult situation for her, but she was rather enthused to do it because she realized the importance of doing so. We sat and talked for a long time until sleep overcame us.

The Fourth Day of the Court

On Thursday morning, we went to the attorney's office. We met the attorney at 8:45 a.m. We walked together to the court. We found the prosecutor and his assistant were both there.

The defense attorney exchanged talks with the prosecutor about the case. They had a display board to display to the jury. This was the final day. Three witnesses were left for testimonies—my wife, her father, and her uncle—according to the attorney's plan and finally the closing.

The attorney read what was written on the board, and she was dismayed. She objected to some of the paragraphs of the text written on the board. The prosecutor and his assistant sat in their assigned seats. Both were whispering together.

As for me, I was speculating. All glory is due to God. A female attorney confronted two male prosecutors for the last four days. She put them in check and caused them several embarrassments. She was defending the case alone with no assistants while both male prosecutors took turns defending their claims. She objected to many of their statements and caused many headaches for both of them. She had a strong proof of evidence, a super presentation, and sound information. All glory is due to God, who granted her strength, patience, a witty mind, and super understanding. She is active, dynamic, and energetic.

I turned to the translator before the judge and jury came into the courtroom and spoke to him with the Lebanese dialect, "I don't want you to sleep today. I want you to be awake and alert." I just joked with him to attract his attention.

The judge and her commission came into the courtroom. The defense attorney took the opportunity and requested a meeting with the judge at the sidebar. When they finished their conversation, the judge met both parties, the prosecutor and defense attorney. The prosecutor angrily carried away his display board . The judge didn't settle with crossing out some of the phrases that were written on the display board but rather requested that the prosecutor cut out the portion of the board where the writing was.

I noticed how upset the prosecutors were. They were totally dissatisfied with this act. In the meantime, the defense attorney happily returned to her seat. The judge ordered the jury to come in. After all the members of the jury took their assigned seats, the talented attorney requested her witness to come to the witness stand. My wife walked to the witness stand with dignity and pride. She sat confidently on her seat.

The attorney threw her questions, and she answered them through the interpreter. The interpreter stumbled a lot in his translations. My wife's testimony was essentially that she was an amateur drawing artist. She presented some of her hand drawings to the court and presented them to the judge and jury. They were impressed with her artistic abilities. She also presented some of her painting tools, among which were the crayons.

All the people in the court were surprised to see all of that. The materials she displayed looked very much like the presented items that were taken out of my backpack. The size was the only difference between the two found items but much smaller.

My wife's testimony included the names of all the people who visited us before my journey. She also talked about packing my backpack for the trip two days prior. The prosecutor directed further questions to her. She looked excellent and convincing despite being bashful. She presented her case excellently, and I can't offer her the appropriate due thanks and gratitude. She was just wonderful.

My wife left the witness stand.

The attorney whispered in my ear, "I'll settle with these witnesses, and I will not call your father-in-law and his brother to the witness stand. But would you sit on the witness stand? The case is going in our favor. But if you took the witness stand, I could easily say that we achieved the best level of success in this trial."

This was the first time the defense attorney expressed her optimistic views. She looked very happy with what had transpired thus far.

I turned to my wife, my family members, and my colleague, and I felt as if they were saying to me, "Go forward, Essam. Be definitely sure of God's victory and success."

The attorney stood up to request Essam AlMohandis to the witness stand. I walked to the stand, thinking of the prayers of my parents, family members, and all the loved ones. I was fully sure that God would grant me full success. I believe that God is just and fair and the full supporter of those who suffer injustice.

I sat down, took the oath, and began answering the attorney's questions. She asked me about my early education background, all the way up to the master stage. She asked me about working with Americans in the King Faisal Specialist Hospital and many other aspects of my life travels and so forth. The questioning lasted for approximately fifteen minutes.

It was the turn of the prosecutor to pose his questions. He questioned me for over thirty minutes. I was the last witness, and he wanted to win the case. The judge warned him not to exceed the time limits by repeating the same questions in different forms.

My attorney raised many objections to the prosecutor's questions. After a lot of debate, playing with words and using various terminologies, the questioning and trial ended with God's help. Thus, my attorney was well alert and prepared to answer every comment he made. All praise is due to God the Almighty.

At the time for the closing remarks, the prosecutor's team reminded the jury with the importance of maintaining the national security of the United States and protection of the Americans. "Everyone who tampers with this should receive a severe punishment." He repeated his statements in several ways until I felt that we had wasted the last four days of litigations on the case. I was frightened. I was under lots of pressures.

On one side, I was afraid, and on the other, I was sure of God's victory and support. I always felt the virtues of my parents' prayers, their support, and kind feelings. I felt the same about my brothers, sisters, uncles, aunts, neighbors, colleagues, and so forth.

The talented attorney stood up and addressed her speech to the jury. "The evidence of the case that was displayed before you and the testimonies you heard, along with the experts' opinions and testimony of the defendant himself, are all before you." She tried to turn their judgment based on the evidence they had heard and seen.

The judge finally gave the opportunity to the jury to start their deliberations. At the end of the case, we all left the courtroom.

We thanked the interpreter for his efforts, and he wished us every success. My father-in-law invited us all for lunch in the same popular restaurant, "the Park." He insisted on the invitation of the attorney and her assistant, along with his law trainee girl. They all joined us for lunch. The attorney was thinking about the conclusion of the case.

The Case at the Hands of the Jury: The Carrier of the Glad Tidings

The attorney said, "The case is turned over to the jury, and they are expected to be here on Thursday evening to give their opinion on it. Based on my previous experience, the deliberation period of the jury may take half the time of the case proceedings. Since the litigation took four days, I expect them to come after two more days."

Thursday passed, and the jury did not come. At 4:30 p.m., the attorney was informed affirmatively that the jury completed their deliberations for that day and they would resume their deliberations tomorrow Friday at 9:00 a.m.

We all came to the attorney's office at 8:00 a.m. on Friday. At about 10:00 a.m., both the prosecutor and defense attorney were called in because the jury wanted to inquire about the first allegation concerning carrying explosive materials onboard the airplane. The answer was given as per the judge's directions. We anticipated hearing their opinion in the case before lunch, but we did not hear anything from them.

At about 1:30 p.m., the prosecutor and the defense attorney were called again to give an answer about the nature of the wrong information given at the interrogation at the airport. They provided an answer to that inquiry as well. At about 4:00 p.m., the attorney's assistant and the law trainee suggested taking some photos together. We went all together to the Atlantic Ocean, as it is located opposite to the Federal Defense Bureau and John Joseph Moakley Courthouse.

We took some photos and walked for a little while by the lake's beach. I got deeply indulged in thinking. I looked at the Atlantic Ocean and talked to myself. I had learned, felt, seen, and believed that the one who salvaged Prophet Abraham PBUH out of the fire as in the Glorious Quran, the Prophets 18:69, said, "O Fire. Be cool and peace onto Abraham. And the One who salvaged Prophet Jonah PBUH while in the belly of the whale." God stated in Quran, Saffat 37:146, "And we grew over him a pumpkin tree." And the one who salvaged Prophet Mohammed PBUH, the master of the progeny of Prophet Adam PBUH from the disbelievers of Korishites and the idolaters of Makkah 15:95, said, "We've sufficed you those who scoff."

I realized that God the Almighty would protect me and salvage me from their plights and evils. I went on praying and asking God seeking His help.

I said, "Oh God, as You have returned Prophet Yuosef PBUH to his father and Prophet Moses PBUH to his mother, please return me soon to my homeland and parents and family. You are the near one, the all-hearing." I went on calling upon God the Almighty. "Oh God, don't make me a trial for the wrongdoers and salvage us with Your mercy from the unjust people."

The response of God the Almighty would come soon. The King of all Kings would salvage me from all worries. He put the quick glad tidings to me as a sign, meeting my wife, her father, her uncle, and my colleague in Boston. He would complete His favor and grand grace unto me by enabling me to meet my parents, my two children, my family, and friends. To Him belongs all the praise, gratitude, and thanks.

My father-in-law asked me, "What are you thinking about?"

I said, "Nothing."

At this point, the attorney's assistant asked me to translate to him what was going on. I turned to him.

Without thinking, I told him, "We shall hear some good news, dear."

I felt as if the ease of the situation were very near. Indeed, not before long, we were informed that the jury had deliberated their decision, and we had to attend to the courtroom in order to hear their opinion. We all walked in the same direction, and one could only hear the sound of our breath and our footsteps on the ground. No one spoke to anyone. We reached the courtroom within only a few minutes.

Along with me, the judge and her commission, the defense attorney, the prosecutor and his assistant, the judge's secretary, my wife, her father, his brother Mr. Saud, and my friend Ossama, all entered the overcrowded courtroom. There were newsmen from the *Herald*, Boston newspapers, and others. There were a number of attorneys from the public defense attorney's office and a team of the FBI and state police officers.

The judge ordered the jury's team that was composed of twelve people to come in. The team was made up of six men and six women. The team came into the courtroom during the litigations. The jury's foreman handed the paper that they had written their decision on to the judge. The paper was in a sealed envelope. I was watching the scene with all my senses.

The judge thanked both parties for the speedy trial in the case that lasted only for eight weeks from beginning to end with all arrangements, coordination, and closing. She also thanked all those who had contributed to the making of all procedures and processions. She further thanked the jury for their efforts that lasted for one consecutive week. Then she reached the envelope that had the decision of the jury, which the jury's foreman delivered to her. As she opened it, I froze still in my place, praying to God the Almighty from the deep of my heart.

The judge raised her voice. "All members of the jury unanimously agreed that Mr. Essam AlMohandis is not guilty on the first charge of carrying explosives onboard the plane." She further added, "All members of the jury unanimously agreed that Mr. Essam

AlMohandis is not guilty on the second charge of providing misleading information on purpose to the customs officer."

At this point, I heard my wife yelling. The sound was a mixture of crying and happy wording. I fell down on the floor to my knees, prostrating to God the Almighty and confessing His grand favor and great bounties. Tears rolled from my eyes heavily. I was overjoyed and happy. It was a very touching scene. All those who were present in the court were touched.

The judge herself quickly left the courtroom. The dream of the female law student came true. I heard the words and statements of the jury members. I noticed their feelings. They all interacted with my case and me. They all had very noble feelings. Even the talented attorney couldn't control herself. My dear, beloved, and loyal wife Ummu Mohammed was also overjoyed. We hugged each other in the court. Both of us were in tears. We cried out of joy and happiness.

We were thankful and grateful to God the Almighty for His perfection and grace. I hugged my father-in-law and his brother. I hugged my colleague Ossama joyfully. I also hugged the attorney's assistant. I received the congratulations of several of the federal defense attorneys, who came to the courtroom as well.

A lady journalist from the *Daily Herald*, one of the oldest and famous newspapers in Boston, came to me and asked me about my feelings. I expressed the state of unfairness and injustice that I felt at the time. The attorney, who had the best hand in declaring my innocence after God, also declared my innocence to the press as well.

I went toward the prosecutor and his assistant, who turned to me and said, "We let you go in order to. See your children and raise them."

The prosecutor's assistant left the courtroom, quickly pulling the tails of defeat and loss. I read that clearly on his face and his harsh words. I could hardly forget that scene.

The prosecutor had a good spirit in spite what he demonstrated in court. He was determined through all his maneuvers to affix the accusations onto me in the courtroom from the beginning of the court proceedings until the end of the sessions when the court's innocence decree was issued.

He posed an implied apology to me. "I was just doing my job. I have no negative feelings or personal grudges against you."

He was polite in his apologies. He wished us a happy life. I also wished him well in his life and career. I even invited him to come visit us at home in the Kingdom of Saudi Arabia, the land of originality, love, and peace. He told me that he knew Saudi Arabia. He had lived and worked there for some time.

I wish, if I could in conversation with the prosecutor's assistance, to let him know that I must not submit myself and become subdued. I should not apologize for a shameful act that he didn't do. A Muslim is a person of principle and should not change my stance from falsehood in spite of all its forces. Verily, God will make a believer victorious..

We are the progeny of a great, eternal, and honorable nation. The others must value that and know it. When we force ourselves as a nation on the rest of the world, we will regain our respect, honor, dignity, and reverence. We do so by seeking knowledge, performing good deeds, applying justice, respecting the dignity of the human being, and applying God's laws, rules, and regulations on all of our affairs. Only then would no one be able to dare to arrest any one of us. He would count to a thousand before doing so. He would not arrest a person for just having crayons in his backpack.

My father-in-law could not wait any longer. He immediately called my parents at home. He informed all my relatives about the court's acquittal. I went along with my attorney to the court's office to remove the electronic monitoring bracelet device, which had stayed on my wrist for the last five weeks.

The court and my suffering ended. My acquittal of all counts in the indictment was publically declared. God the Almighty defeated the plots of all conniving people. They were equally rewarded. The puzzling question remained. Who did it? Who was the sinning criminal person who placed these items in my backpack? Who wanted to criminalize me for no harm or sin I committed? Why would he not be accountable for his evil action?

The litigations of the court ended, and the true criminal person who placed those items in my backpack was not tried. However, I entrust such a person's affair to God the Almighty. He was about to put me in the dark depths of jails God only knows for how long. But on the Day of Judgment, God the Almighty would surely account such a criminal.

We left the fences of the John Joseph Moakley Courthouse. On our way, I met some members of the jury.

One commented jokingly, "Go home and enjoy your lives."

The newspaper cameras took pictures of us.

The revered attorney told me, "You are a free man. Go do as you like. But don't make your reservations until next Monday in order to obtain the judgment of acquittal and collect the bond money."

We all went to the Federal Defense Office along with the attorney. My colleague Ossama and my wife's uncle went to the airport, as they insisted to stay until they heard the decision of the court themselves. They wanted to share our happiness with us.

We said good-bye to the revered professional attorney and wished her a calm and beautiful weekend with no worries or disturbances. I walked along with my wife and her father, wandering on foot in Boston's streets. We went later to the hotel where my father-in-law was staying. We had good times together. At about 10:00 p.m., I took leave to go to my apartment. He requested us to stay with him in the same hotel, but I informed him that I wanted to pack and check out from the apartment.

I informed him that we would come to the hotel and spend the day together tomorrow. We had an appointment with the attorney on Monday to conclude the remaining procedures and make reservations to go back home. He kindly walked with us to the hotel's gate. We promised to see him again in the morning.

The Second Arrest: What Happened?

For the first time, I felt hungry and had a real desire to eat something since two months. We had dinner, and we headed to the apartment where we were staying. We were close to the Perdentall Mall. I talked to my wife about the mall and promised to take her there.

I told my wife, "All glory is due to God. It was Friday when I was forced to be under home arrest, and it was also Friday when I was announced innocent. All praise is due to God the Almighty."

Friday is a blessed day for Muslims. We picked out some needed items from a grocery shop in the neighborhood, and we walked to the apartment building. The streets were still alive. Car traffic was still on the roads. People were waiting for the weekend. We passed by a number of homeless drunkards on the way. We came across a number of aimless youth who were wandering on the streets.

I entered the apartment while the phone was ringing. A friend of mine was calling from home to congratulate me and share my happiness with me. After I concluded the call with my friend, I heard a knock at the door. I was worried. I didn't expect any visitors at that time. I hid my feelings from my wife. I thought it might be a person ringing the door by mistake. It was almost 1:00 a.m. A few seconds later, the phone was ringing.

I heard a command, "Open the door at once."

Seven people were holding guns right in front of my face. I put my hands up while looking toward my wife. She was shocked and frightened from such a scene. I had never been in a similar situation in my life, except in Hollywood's movies. I was a simple, unarmed person.

"What have I done? I was declared innocent today in the court."

"We have an order to arrest you. We've been waiting for you since six p.m."

I didn't know who they were. They ordered me to go with them. I gave my wallet to my wife, and when I was about to go with them, the phone rang again. I reached the handset of the telephone.

"Hello, my brother Yousef ."

"Congratulations."

"Please call the attorney and inform her that seven unknown officials arrested me again and my wife is alone in the apartment."

The officers pulled the handset from my hand and placed the handcuffs on my wrists.

My wife kept on calling me. "Essam, what should I do?"

I couldn't say even a word. I was choked. My tongue was tied. The events were so quick. These events took a toll on me. I was forced into the black armored vehicle. The vehicle parked in front of a big building after almost fifteen minutes of its move. The gate was automatically opened. The vehicle entered the parking area, and the gate was automatically closed again. I was taken inside the building.

They took my fingerprints and photos again. I sat on a steel seat for some time. They handed me a white uniform to wear. I put them on and went back to my seat. I didn't know why I was brought there. And I didn't know either what they wanted from me. I was worried about my wife and how would she behave. I didn't know what she felt about such a savage and heartbreaking invasion of my privacy. After an hour, the officer in charge informed me that there was a visitor to see me. I thought it might be my attorney. I was surprised.

"Oh God, the prosecutor. What brings you here?"

"Mr. Essam, I am sorry for what happened. Believe me, I did not do this. It was someone else."

"What happened to my wife?"

It was as if he felt the amount of horror I had. "Don't worry. Your wife went to the Perdentall Mall after you left. Fortunately, she met a kind man, and she gave him the attorney's business card. He called her, and she immediately sent her assistant to her."

His words comforted me. He informed me that she was now with her father in the hotel and she was fine.

"All praise is due to God the Almighty. Where am I? What is this place?"

"You are in the deportation facilities since your entry visa to the USA was revoked."

"How long would I stay here? When they would deport me?"

"I shall do my best to expedite your deportation procedures, and I promise to send you tomorrow Saturday if there is a flight."

Before he left, he handed me his business card with all his contacts, including his residence phone. He apologized again and left the place.

After a short while, a largely built officer came to see me. "I'll take you to the clinic."

"Why? I don't have any complaints."

"This is a normal check-up procedure for every person who comes to this place."

We walked from place to place and from building to building until we reached the clinic. After the check-up, he returned me to the first building where he escorted me.

While he was locking the gate, he turned to me and said, "I am sure that you are not going to escape or run away."

I looked at him with a pitying smile on my face. "How would I escape or run away from you while you surround me from everywhere?" I meant that he was a large-bodied person. He looked back at me with a victory smile on his face. He liked what I had said.

The officer led me into a large hall. We went through the hall to a ward where there were over twenty other persons. I took my assigned place and sat down. One of the inmates introduced himself to me. He said he was from Brazil. We talked for a long time until 4:00 a.m.

I was so tired. I leaned to the wall while sitting on my steel bed, which reminded me of the days I spent in the PCCF. I opened my eyes and noticed that it was 6:00 a.m. I got up, performed my ablution, and offered my dawn prayers. I went to one of the small windows that looked out at the streets, looking to the vehicles crossing the highway. The ward was distinct because it had separate bathroom facilities. A wall clock was at the end of the ward. Even the officers in charge in the deportation were friendlier and less strict. Handcuffs weren't applied when moving from one place to another.

It was 6:30 a.m., time for breakfast. We all moved to the main hall. Every person was given a breakfast utensil. All members were seated at four-people tables. I sat with the rest of the people, but I did not take anything to eat. At 7:00 a.m., everyone was ordered to get back to his places in the ward after the breakfast.

As soon as I settled down in my place, I heard my name being called. I went along with the officer. He requested me to change my clothes and go with him. He said we were going to Logan International Airport. They wanted to deport me to my home country.

"No one is able to appreciate his home country except those who are forced to leave it. Don't you ever think that our home country is a toy in our hands or a word that we write in a field on our passport? Its task is not to pass borders to other countries or travel over continents. A homeland is far more important than gambling with it. You should realize why people sacrifice their lives for their countries. A homeland country is synonymous to the sense of belonging. It grows up with us. It makes us feel our values as humans. The homeland country lives inside us and not merely we live in it. Therefore, we always seek a homeland country that makes us feel our values as humans and live in it in peace, today and tomorrow where we live an honorable life."[14]

---

[14]   Zainab Haqqui

I got on their vehicle while shackles and handcuffs on my wrists were still on me. This was the first time I rode in their car with a feeling of happiness, but it was mixed with a touch of worries for my wife and my father-in-law.

I was asked to get out of the car, and I was taken through Logan International Airport terminals until we reached the secondary inspection zone that I passed through when I arrived in the United States on January 3, 2004.

Returning to the Homeland

Passengers started coming to Frankfurt airport three hours before the departure of the plane. I saw many of my country's citizens at the airport. They had bright faces. I missed my homeland country. I missed every breeze that came from it. We lined up before the airlines officer waiting for boarding passes. I took my seat on the plane, and the doors were locked. The plane moved to the runway. I wondered while looking in the sky. We listened to the flight's instructions, and we heard the "Travel Supplication" read in a warm voice. I could not help but cry with tears. The supplications were in Arabic. I wiped my tears of happiness.

The flight to Jeddah would take approximately five hours. I felt comforted and happy. I was happy on board the Saudi airlines that carry the warm desert colors. The only thing interrupting my sleep was thinking of my country and my family members.

Only a few hours remained to join my beloved family at home. I missed my homeland country. I wanted to enjoy every scene therein. I was truly deprived of the scenes of my country for no sin I committed. I truly miss you, my homeland country. You are the pleasure of my eyes and heart. We shall meet after a long separation.

While I was dozing off, I heard the airplane pilot announcing that we were flying over the western coastal area of Jeddah. We were actually over the Jeddah commercial seaport. It was a wonderful scene. The lights of Jeddah, the bride of the Red Sea, were visible.

I fixed my eyes on the scene. I didn't move neither left nor right. I had known this great city very well. I had known the squares, fountains, main buildings, and glorious history of Jeddah. How beautiful was the scenes and city itself. The lights of the city mixed with the sound of the Red Sea waves. It was marvelous.

The plane landed on the runway of King AbdulAziz International Airport at Jeddah. I entered the terminal, and I breathed the original traditions of Jeddah, its history, and its special essence. Jeddah has an impression that is only known to those who lived in its streets, alleys, and so forth. It is only known to those who realize the simplicity of its dwellers.

We headed to the passport queue. Then we went on to the domestic terminal to take the flight going to Riyadh. We spent an hour and twenty minutes. It was the longest hour in my entire life. I wanted to land in the great city of Riyadh. As soon as the plane's doors were opened for us to get off the plane, I ran my legs off. The earth was unable to carry me. I was attracted by love and longing to my home, family, and all. I was counting on meeting my loved ones. I climbed down the escalators of King Khalid International Airport to meet my beloved brother, Yousef.

We hugged each other for a long time. Here was my dear and beloved father. There were my dear and beloved paternal uncles and aunts. There were my beloved brothers, friends, and other family member. All had a smile of happiness on their faces. You could see the loyalty and true love on their faces. It was a gorgeous reception by all. Everyone wished me well and offered me their best congratulations. It was a lovely and nice thing.

I hugged both of my parents, who did not stop for a second offering their supplications and good prayers to God the Almighty for me. They were thankful and grateful to God the Almighty for His grace and blessings.

I met many of my friends and colleagues. I don't know how to thank them all. I can't offer them the praise and thanks they all deserve. I was lost for words. I can't forget their noble feelings and emotions. I shall remember all their kindness and love forever. The tongues were incapable of speaking what I needed to express to all of those. Again, I was lost for words. I could not find in my vocabulary enough words to express my feelings toward all those who stood by me in this trial.

The parade went through the streets of the city of Riyadh, the capitol of the Kingdom of Saudi Arabia. It was like a virgin bride being escorted to her loving and longing bridegroom. How beautiful and great is the homeland country.

We drove through the streets of Riyadh, enjoying the aroma and breeze. It was 12:00 p.m. on Saturday night. As for my wife and her father, they were on their way to Heathrow Airport in London, returning to the homeland. I shall be at the airport to receive them there later on Sunday evening.

Upon their return, I would close a page of suffering and remove a period of a dark injustice and unfairness. The sun of truth shall rise after false and plain aggression. The high cry of the truth is heard loud and clear by everyone all over. The lights of peace, justice, and love set down and would never rise up from the West again.

Yes, I had learned, felt, seen, and believed that the person who is conscious of God the Almighty would see that He would make him a way out and provide him with means from sources he would think the least he would be able to get from. God the Almighty granted me strength after weakness. He granted me security after being frightened. He granted me provisions after being poor. For me, God the Almighty employed those who did and did not know me. All—whether they were Christians, Jews, or else—helped and assisted me.

I kept on calling and invoking upon the King of all Kings, God the Almighty, and He kept on assisting and helping me. God stated in Quran, Surah Chapter The Ants 29:62, "Or, Who listens to the (soul) distressed when it calls on Him, and Who relieves its suffering, and makes you (mankind) inheritors of the earth? (Can there be another) god besides God? Little it is that you heed." I raised my hand up to Him. He didn't return them empty out of His generosity and kindness bashfulness.

I had learned, felt, seen, and believed that there is an ease with the difficulty. Never a difficulty conquers two eases.

All praise is due to God the Almighty by whose
Name all goods are completed.
May God's peace and blessings be unto His prophet and
slave-servant Messenger Mohammed PBUH.

Special Thanks

Dr. Anwar AlJaberti, Professor Amin Kashmiri, Dr. Sultan AlSudairi, Dr. Mohammed AlSamman, Dr. Fatwan AlMohanna, Dr. Ahmad AlBarrak, Dr. Mohammed AlHarithi, Mr. Saad AlHasan, Mr. Hasan Mighfar, Engineer Ahmad Saleh, Dr. Mohammed AbaHusain, Engineer Abdullah AlRasheed, Engineer Abdullah AlDubaib, Engineer Mohammed AlSuwailim, Engineer Sultan AlRomayyan, Engineer Salama Rahma, Mr. Mohammed AlSharekh, Engineer Rami Hijazi, and Mr. Muaddee AlSurayye'

A clipping from an interview with *Arab News* newspaper

القضاء الأمريكي يبرئ
السعودي عصام المهندس

بوسطن: أ ب

برأ محلفون فيدراليون
السعودي عصام محمد المهندس
(33 عاماً) من تهمة حمله لمواد
حارقة على متن رحلة كانت قادمة
من السعودية مروراً بألمانيا قبل
أن تحط في مطار لوقان الدولي في
مدينة بوسطن، كما برئ المهندس
من تهمة الإدلاء بمعلومات خاطئة
للمسؤولين الأمريكيين في المطار
أثناء وصوله. وأبدى المهندس
امتنانه لهيئة المحلفين التي
اتخذت القرار ببراءته يوم أول من
أمس.

وكانت محامية المهندس
(مريم كونراد) قد ذكرت أن موكلها
قد تم استهدافه بطريقة غير عادلة
في المطار. وقالت إن موكلها ''ليس
إرهابياً. مثله مثل (بابا الفاتيكان)
يوحنا بولس الثاني''.

أخبار News

ASHARQ AL-AWSAT
الشرق الأوسط
Issue 9231 العدد Sunday 2004/3/7 الاحد

السعودي الذي اعتقل في أميركا بتهمة حيازة مفرقعات نارية: محامية يهودية برأتني

الرياض: موفق النويصر

كشف السعودي عصام محمد البيتي المتخصص في صيانة الأجهزة الطبية، وأرشد الأميركية من قبل مستشفى أنك فيصل التخصصي ومركز الأبحاث لرفض لمصدر دورة تكفلها نواة الأجهزة الطبية المتطورة تفاصيل عملية وقع الشك من خطر معك من سفيدن، وكيف أسيئت معاملة الثلاثي داخل حليمة البحرية بعد خلال 21 يوما قضاها هناك قبل أن يطلق سراحه بكفالة 90 ألف ريال [25 ألف دولار]، ولارتباط الإقامة الصيبة الأميركية، وإيداعه السجن ضمن في بلاده تحت الرقابة الإلكترونية.

يمهد البلندس في مسار رفع التهمة لمصدر دورة تكفلها نواة الشرق الأوسط أن عمانية يهودية تحمينه من قبل المحكمة الأميركية القضاء من عنك معاملة من قبل المحكمة من بلاده أنه أخذه الهجرة باستمالة وسمحة ثم بمجمع كافة التهم التي أسند ضده واتبع تلعب عقوبتها في حال الإدانة في السجون كما عاما يقارب 950 ألف ريال [250 ألف دولار].

يبرد البلندس الفصل الثاني من رحلة عباده بعد أن برأته المحكمة عندما أوضح أنني العام لسلطات الهجرة باستمالة وسمحة ومن لم توجهه إلى السعودية، على كرم من سريان مفعول تأشيرته ونحوله لولايات المتحدة قبل يهود أي حكم بإبعاده شده. [تفاصيل ص 4]

4

أخبار News

ASHARQ AL-AWSAT   8

Issue 9231 مدت Sunday 2004/3/7

السعودي عصام المهندس يروي لـ«الشرق الأوسط» معاناة شهرين قضاهما
في بوسطن بدأت باعتقاله بتهمة عقوبتها السجن 15 سنة وانتهت بتبرئته

Essam Al-Mohandis Tells All About His Ordeal in US

Muwaffak Al-Nuwaiser
Asharq Al-Awsat

RIYADH — Essam Muhammad Al-Mohandis, a Saudi biomedical engineer recently acquitted in the US of smuggling explosives, has described the vindictive behavior of US immigration authorities.

In an exclusive interview, Al-Mohandis, an employee of King Faisal Specialist Hospital and Research Center in Riyadh, spoke of how federal agents maltreated him during his ordeal.

He said his lawyer Miriam Conrad was successful in disproving all the charges against him. The charges — possession and smuggling of explosives and lying to Customs authorities — were enough to sentence him for 15-year prison with a fine of SR950,000 ($250,000).

Al-Mohandis was arrested for carrying three small sparklers on a flight from Germany to Boston.

Al-Mohandis, who had flown to Boston for a five-day training seminar on how to use DNA equipment purchased by the Riyadh hospital, said he never thought his journey would end in a US prison for dangerous criminals.

US police arrested him again eight hours after his acquittal for not having a valid visa. Al-Mohandis did not have a current visa because the federal officers had revoked his visa after the arrest.

"While I was receiving congratulations for the acquittal, seven gun-wielding security officers came to our hotel room and asked me to escort them. They told me they were from the Immigration Department," he said.

He said the officers did not allow him to call either his lawyer or his father. "They did not even allow me to take my clothes. They later took me to the deportation cell, where I was treated much better," he said.

He said prosecuting US Attorney Gregory Moffatt collected his wallet and credit cards and brought them to him in jail, along with a personal apology. "He said the decision to arrest him was taken by a colleague," he said.

The Customs officials in Boston also called him for a meeting before his departure for Riyadh. They asked him several questions including whether he was afraid of returning to the Kingdom and whether he had any problems with the Saudi government. "I told them no."

* * *

(Read the full report in tomorrow's Arab News)

Tuesday, March 9, 2004   **Kingdom • Gulf**   arab news

Someone Put the Sparklers in My Bag: Mohandis

*Muwaffek Al-Nuwaiser
Asharq Al-Awsat*

RIYADH — Essam Al-Mohandis, the Saudi who spent 21 days in a US jail for alleged possession of explosives, has told his story in this exclusive interview with Asharq Al-Awsat, a sister publication of Arab News.

The King Faisal Specialist Hospital and Research Center in Riyadh, where Al-Mohandis is in charge of medical equipment, had asked him to attend a training course in Boston at short notice, and he was booked on a Lufthansa flight via Frankfurt.

Mohandis says he met a colleague at Riyadh Airport on Jan. 3. "While we were at the Riyadh airport we went through four security checks," he said. After arriving in Frankfurt, Al-Mohandis and the colleague toured the duty-free shops inside the airport for two hours. "At Frankfurt I was checked thoroughly again by German security officers and they allowed me to board the plane," he said.

After arriving in Logan airport in Boston he queued for nearly one-and-a-half hours to complete immigration procedures. "When they called me for the interview, an officer asked me politely to leave the bag outside. Another officer later interviewed me and asked me several questions. He asked me about the purpose of my visit, the nature of the course, the tentative period of my stay, my work and the type of equipment I would be trained to use and about the hospital where I work."

After the interview Al-Mohandis moved to the Customs department where they checked the visa and asked him to put his baggage on the X-ray machine. They asked me two specific questions: whether I carried more than $10,000 and did anybody give me anything to take into the country. I told them no."

The officer then inspected his bag and found some personal items, some brochures related to the course, and a book on linguistics which he was reading on the plane. "In the meantime, the officer took out some small tubes from the pocket of the suitcase. They were yellow and marked K0201. They asked me what this was, and I told them they could be wax crayons."

Al-Mohandis thought that his wife, who is an artist, might have kept them in the bag. "I asked the officer to allow me to check them to see what exactly they were, but he asked me not to touch them. One of the tubes, which was in the hands of the

Essam Al-Mohandis with his father Muhammad Al-Mohandis. (AN photo)

officer, was broken and a brown powder came out it. I thought they were drugs and it really frightened me. The officer again asked him what is this? I did not answer because I really did not know what they were and where they came from."

Al-Mohandis was taken to the head of the Customs department who asked him several questions, and authorities detained Al-Mohandis in a room alone while the Customs chief, the head of the FBI and national security officers held a meeting in the next room. Then they started questioning him for six hours after reading out the charges against him. He told them that he was ready to answer their questions without a lawyer. They asked him to contact his father and wife but he told them he did not want to do so because it would upset them. However, he agreed to inform the Saudi Embassy in Washington. But his refusal to inform his father and wife was taken as an attempt to hide vital information. "Then they told me I was under arrest."

After spending a night at the police station, Al-Mohandis was taken to court. Before that he had met with his court appointed attorney, Miriam Conrad. The judge told Al-Mohandis that US Attorney General Gregory Moffatt had two charges against him: Possession of explosives on board the plane and lying to the Customs authorities.

Al-Mohandis was put in the Plymouth County Correctional Facility, 40 km from Boston, in the C category, which is allocated for dangerous criminals. While a police officer was completing procedures

at the jail, he saw a television report on the man's arrest and this changed his attitude toward him, Al-Mohandis believes.

The guard first put him in an isolated cell and later took him to another cell which was extremely cold and took all Al-Mohandis' clothes except his trousers. "They kept me there for 14 hours. I asked them why they were keeping me in such a cell. They said they were afraid I was hiding explosives in my stomach. They later gave me clothes and put me in another isolation cell with a security camera."

During this time, Conrad and her team were trying to get him released without bail. The public prosecutor insisted on bail of $50,000 and a bond from Saudi authorities. But the lawyer was able to convince the judge to release Al-Mohandis on condition that he would wear an electronic tag, which allowed him movement only within five meters of a designated area. The authorities allowed him to go out shopping once in a week for three hours.

A trial date was set for one month later. The lawyer was able to convince the judge to issue an order for the US Embassy in Riyadh to expedite visas for the defense witnesses. The court also agreed to pay the expenses of the witnesses — his wife, her father, uncle and wife of the uncle and his superior and colleague.

Security authorities in San Francisco had sent the colleague back to Riyadh after putting him in jail for a week for traveling with Al-Mohandis on the same flight. The FBI also questioned an American who sat near Al-Mohandis' on the plane.

Al-Mohandis' father meanwhile met with Prince Muhammad Ibn Naif, assistant interior minister for security affairs, in Riyadh and told him the story. Prince Muhammad offered him all his support, and the Saudi Embassy in Washington notified Al-Mohandis after two weeks that they had received a confidential note from the Interior Ministry.

During the five-day trial, the public prosecution presented their witnesses including the customs officers and an explosive expert. "Their answers were contradictory. I looked at the Customs officer who accused me of lying. He was trying to avoid looking at me," Al-Mohandis said, adding this might have created doubts about the officer's truthfulness.

The explosives expert also failed to give correct information as he exaggerated the weight of explosives is one of the tubes found on Al-Mohandis. Defense witnesses also included an explosives expert, who was able to persuade the court that the two tubes were in fact sparklers and unlikely to be harmful. Al-Mohandis' wife submitted a number of her drawings to the court to show that his guess that the tubes were crayons had not been fanciful.

The colleague who had been on the same flight confirmed that they had both gone through several security checks. "This proves that (the sparklers) were put in my bag during the eight minutes when I left the bag outside the Customs room," he said.

Al-Mohandis left the courtroom on Feb. 19 at 11 a.m. The next day, the jurors acquitted him of both charges.

A letter addressed to HRH Minister of Foreign Affairs issued by the hospital administration

2/01 2004 17:23 FAX 96614427732   CLINICAL ENGG   ☒001

KINGDOM OF SAUDI ARABIA

**KING FAISAL SPECIALIST HOSPITAL
AND RESEARCH CENTRE**

المملكة العربية السعودية

مستشفى الملك فيصل التخصصي
ومركز الأبحاث

بسم الله الرحمن الرحيم

صاحب السمو الملكي الأمير سعود الفيصل وزير الخارجية   حفظه الله

السلام عليكم ورحمة الله وبركاته

أما بعد ...

قال الله تعالى في حكم تنزيله ﴿ هل جزاء الإحسان إلا الإحسان ﴾

نرفع إلى سموكم الكريم هذا الخطاب بشأن الموظف/ عصام محمد المهندس والذي أرسل من قبل مستشفى الملك فيصل التخصصي ومركز الأبحاث إلى الولايات المتحدة الأمريكية لحضور تدريب على صيانة بعض الأجهزة الطبية وقد قبض عليه هناك بسبب وجود ألعاب نارية في حقيبته وهو أحد الموظفين بالمستشفى في قسم الهندسة الطبية منذ ما يقارب ثمان سنوات حيث كانت حصيلته خلال هذه السنوات أن كسب حب واحترام وتقدير جميع من حوله ومن تعامل معه واحاطته من سعوديين وغير السعوديين، وهو واحد أنشط وأكفأ الموظفين في هذا القسم بشهادة جميع رؤسائه وزملائه وكل من تعامل معه بصفة شخصية أو رسمية داخل وخارج المستشفى، وهو موظف فوق مستوى الشبهات حيث انه إنسان مستقيم يخاف الله ويراقبه في عمله وليس به يوما الى اي ميول منحرفة او متطرفة سواء دينية او سياسية او حتى اجتماعية.

وبعد التحقيقات وسلطة انه لا بد من غرامة كفالة مالية قدرها ٥٠٠٠٠ دولار أمريكي، لذا نود ابلاغكم بأن مستشفى الملك فيصل التخصصي ومركز الأبحاث سيقوم بدفع جميع التكاليف اللازمة او اي ضمانات اخرى مترتبة على هذه القضية وصادرة من المحكمة وذلك اهتماما ورعاية وتقديرا من المستشفى لموظفيه الأكفاء.

لذا نرجو من سموكم توجيه من يلزم لسرعة البت في الموضوع، علما بانه يجب دفع المبلغ المذكور قبل يوم الثلاثاء ٢٠٠٤/١/١٢ م (موعد جلسة المحكمة) وذلك لتسهيل اجراءات اطلاق سراحه وعودته الى أرض الوطن، بإذن الله، ونشكر لسموكم ما عهدناه منكم من رعاية واهتمام بابناء هذا الوطن.

والله يرعاكم.

الدكتور/ عبد المجيد نظيف
المستشار والمشرف على أصول الإدارة
مستشفى الملك فيصل التخصصي ومركز الأبحاث

برق : التخصصي   طلفون : ٧٢٧٢-٤٦٤ (١-٩٦٦) ، ٤٨٣٩-٤٤١ (١-٩٦٦) فاكس ، تلكس : ٤٠١٠٥٠: RYSPEC SJ ، ص . ب : ٣٣٥٤ ، الرياض ١١٢١١
Cable : Specialist   Telephone : (966-1) 464-7272   Fax : (966-1) 441-4839   Telex : 401050: RYSPEC SJ   P.O. Box 3354, Riyadh: 11211
Form810-14 (Rev. 06-16)   I.C. 202048

A photo in the Federal Defense Bureau with the attorney's assistant

A photo after a lunch at Red Lobster, "The Park"
My father-in-law to the right, my colleague Ossama Abbass, Essam AlMohandis, and Saud AlRehan, the uncle of my wife

What urged me to jot down what I had written in this little novel are the lessons that I have learned from the grand Life's University. I had benefited from the experiences that I learned. Some specific points are clearly pointed and i am sure you would be able to grasp what is between the lines!

Yes. I had learned, felt, seen and believed that the person who is conscious of Allah, the Almighty, He would make him a way out and provide him with means from sources he would think the least he would be able to get from. Allah, the Almighty granted me strength after weakness. He granted me security after being frightened. He granted me provisions after being poor. Allah, the Almighty employed for me those who knew me and those who don't know me!. I kept on calling and invoking upon the King of all kings; Lord. I raised my hand up to Him. He didn't return them empty out of His generosity and kindness.

Some of the most beautiful moments are those which man spends with his own thoughts and memories that he lives second by second as he feels their sweetness, bitterness, hopes, pains, pleasures and sorrows, and all their details.

As I jot down what I could of such moments and capture them [by words and phrases], I beg your pardon and ask your forgiveness. I don't mean to excite you and stir your emotions through a novelist writing, but rather, I would like to give an [honest] account of my own story that carries my own emotions and feelings.

I seek your permission to sail with me in order to narrate to you, and in order to see with your own eyes the events of two months of suffering and pains that I spent in the USA, in the state of Massachusetts, in the city of Boston.